E 7/level·

AFRICA

AND

SOME WORLD PROBLEMS

OXFORD UNIVERSITY PRESS
AMEN HOUSE, E.C. 4
LONDON EDINBURGH GLASGOW
LEIPZIG NEW YORK TORONTO
MELBOURNE CAPETOWN BOMBAY
CALCUTTA MADRAS SHANGHAI
HUMPHREY MILFORD
PUBLISHER TO THE
UNIVERSITY

AFRICA

AND

SOME WORLD PROBLEMS

INCLUDING

THE RHODES MEMORIAL LECTURES

DELIVERED IN MICHAELMAS TERM, 1929

BY

GENERAL J. C. SMUTS

OXFORD
AT THE CLARENDON PRESS
1930

Printed in Great Britain

PREFATORY NOTE

THIS booklet consists of addresses delivered during November 1929. The first address was given before the Royal Scottish Geographical Society at Edinburgh and Glasgow on 21 and 22 November. The second, third, and fourth were the Rhodes Memorial Lectures delivered in the Sheldonian Theatre at Oxford on the 2, 9, and 16 November. The fifth is a speech made at a meeting of the League of Nations Union in the Guildhall, London, on 14 November to celebrate the tenth anniversary of the League. And the sixth was delivered as the Sidgwick Memorial Lecture in Newnham College, Cambridge, on 30 November.

J. C. S.

OXFORD
December 1929

CONTENTS

I

LIVINGSTONE AND AFTER

LIVINGSTONE AND AFTER

LET me begin by thanking the Royal Scottish Geographical Society of Edinburgh for their kind invitation which has brought me here. I fear I shall not be able to add appreciably to the geographical knowledge of such a nation of travellers as the Scots. But at any rate I have the opportunity of seeing Scotland again—the Scots I see anywhere—and of revisiting this great city which did me such signal honour in the years of the Great War. I have come here partly to discharge this long-standing debt of gratitude. The debt, however, goes beyond the reception and the honours of twelve years ago. In a sense it is not personal but national. For South Africans can never forget, and will never forget, what Scotland and Scots have done and meant for them. South Africa owes you a very exceptional and special debt for your great contribution to her development and progress. It would be difficult to do adequate justice to the work which Scotsmen have done in the upbuilding of our young country. Your special contribution has consisted not so much in your wares and manufactures as in your manhood. You have exported to us—as indeed you have exported so liberally to many other young countries—your greatest asset: your character, talent, genius. Your national character, like your theology, has left an ineffaceable impress on South Africa. It is often

difficult to know where the Scots end and the Dutch
begin. Between the English and the Dutch in South
Africa you have been a strong link, a bond of understanding and sympathy and good humour. Like St.
Paul, and probably from his Epistles, you have
learnt to be all things to all men; and in a country of
sharp contrasts and keen bargainers like South
Africa you have been the honest broker who has
helped both, and not forgotten himself. For these
and other innumerable services we owe you a deep
debt of gratitude.

But there is one service above all others which you
have rendered South Africa, or rather let me say
Southern Africa: I mean your gift to us of David
Livingstone. Livingstone was not only our greatest
explorer, and the greatest explorer ever produced by
Scotland, he was also our greatest propagandist.
With Rhodes he was one of the two men who did
more in the past to spread the name and fame of
Southern Africa than probably any others. He taught
the world that our sub-continent existed, and his
plain unvarnished report seemed such wild romance
that Africa almost immediately became the Mecca of
the adventurous spirits from every part of the world.
Livingstone placed us in the limelight and we have
been there ever since. We are no longer the Dark
Continent. Beyond this superb advertisement which
he gave us, he made geographical discoveries which
have placed his name among the select few in that
class. He lifted the veil from Southern Africa, and
added more to the knowledge of her mysterious in-

terior than perhaps any other man has done. In recognition of his work the great National Memorial will be erected to his memory near the Victoria Falls in the near future; and the few words I am going to say to-day are largely intended to foreshadow that event, to draw attention to it, and to set men thinking once more of the great hero who gave his life for knowledge: the great humanitarian who more than any one else can claim the honour of having abolished African slavery: the great Christian whose character and example made the natives of Africa believe that the white men were gods and not men of the same clay as themselves. The white man's prestige in Africa is, alas, no longer what it was; but it has proved the greatest moral force in the betterment of Africa, and it was in a large measure due to the enormous impression which Livingstone made on the natives from one end of the sub-continent to the other. You will remember the tribute which the hard and cold Stanley paid to his character after having lived with him in close intimacy for months in the wilds. And you can imagine the impression which his extraordinarily noble personality must have made on the simple African savages.

'A character', says Stanley, 'that I venerated, that called forth all my enthusiasm and sincerest admiration. You may take any point in Dr. Livingstone's character, and analyse it carefully, and I will challenge any man to find a fault in it. His religion is a constant, earnest, sincere practice. It is neither demonstrative nor loud, but manifests itself in a quiet practical way, and is always at work. In him religion exhibits its loveliest features; it governs his conduct, not only towards his servants, but towards the natives, the bigoted Mahomedans, and all who come in contact with him. Without it, Livingstone, with his ardent temperament, his enthusiasm, his high spirit and courage, must have become uncompanionable and a hard master. Religion has tamed him and made him a Christian gentleman, the most companionable of men and indulgent of masters.'[1]

It has always been to me a source of regret that he fell out with the Transvaal Boers and never had a good word to say about them. I once took the opportunity to discuss the matter with President Kruger, and his explanation of the differences which arose between the Boers and Livingstone was that Gordon Cumming—another of your errant countrymen—had supplied the border tribes with rifles and ammunition in exchange for ivory, and that the Boers, finding the natives armed, concluded—erroneously—that Livingstone had done so, and treated him accordingly. For this rough treatment I made some small amends after sixty years when I was a Transvaal Minister, and the remains of Livingstone's mission station at Mabotsa were discovered in the Transvaal. I had the ruins restored as far as possible, and fenced in, and put in charge of the local native chief to look after and care for: in that way a record is still preserved of the place where he spent two happy years with his bride, Mary Moffat. After that small attention and this lecture I hope his implacable spirit against my people will at last relent.

On the 1st of June 1849 Livingstone set forth

---

[1] *How I found Livingstone*, pp. 430, 434.

from his Bechuana mission station on that career of discovery which was to carry him to Lake Ngami in that year, and ultimately to the glorious end on Lake Bangweolo twenty-four years after. Before we proceed to look at his work, let us pause and ask what was then known of the interior of Africa. Of the interior of North Africa our very scanty knowledge at that time was almost entirely due to the amazing journeys in the eighteenth and the beginning of the nineteenth centuries of three other Scotsmen: Mungo Park, who travelled and was eventually killed in the region of the Upper Niger; Laing, who crossed the Sahara from Tripoli to Timbuktu and was killed by the Touarek of the Sahara; and Bruce, who explored in the region of Abyssinia and the Blue Nile. At the same time that Livingstone started in the south, Henry Barth started from Tripoli across the Sahara, discovered Lake Chad, explored the surrounding territories and rivers, and then marched through Hausaland to the Niger; whence, after further amazing travels he turned back to Tripoli and England. His great discoveries, recorded in five volumes, place him in the very front rank of African travellers. On the East Coast the missionaries Krapf and Rebmann were exploring the country behind Mombasa, and in 1848 first saw Kilimanjaro and, in the following year, Mount Kenya; while they heard vague rumours of the great lakes farther west, and there was the ancient, still vaguer rumour of the Mountains of the Moon in the interior. In South-West Africa Francis Galton and Andersson—the latter to become famous for his subsequent Kalahari travels—were at that time exploring the country behind Walfish Bay, without, however, getting as far as Lake Ngami. This, little as it is, was in substance the extent of our knowledge of the interior of Africa when Livingstone started on his first journey. The vast Congo basin was a sealed book, Eastern and Central Africa with its lakes and volcanoes, its rift valleys and rivers, was quite unknown; the Zambesi was known to the Portuguese as far as Tete, and there was some vague knowledge through Jesuit missionaries of Mashonaland with its kingdom of Monomotapa, its gold mines, and its ancient ruins. The map of the African interior still looked like a picture of a menagerie rather than a piece of geography. It is strange to think that eighty years ago this was still the extent of our knowledge of the interior of Africa—apart from the territory occupied by whites in the south, and Egypt and the Mediterranean regions of the north. Thirty years after, a revolution in our knowledge of African geography had been brought about; except for details the vast framework of its lakes, its rivers, and its mountain systems was fully known. The work in Southern and South-central Africa was done almost single-handed and with the slenderest resources by Livingstone, while to the north of him a whole array of geographical genius, equipped in many cases on a lavish scale, was carrying on the great work.

Let us look for a moment at the steps in Livingstone's explorations and discoveries. He had laid the foundations of his future task by acquiring the rudiments of a scientific training at Glasgow, by learning the accurate use of the necessary instruments for taking the latitude and longitude of places, and by eight years of assiduous study, as a missionary in Bechuanaland, of the native languages and customs and the native mentality. He was naturally very observant and careful in his use of language and descriptions of what he saw. The result was that his books, apart from his geographical discoveries and their interest as a great traveller's story, were mines of accurate information. Professor Passarge, the Leipzig geographer and geologist who spent some time in the investigation of the geology of the Kalahari, places him first in importance of all Kalahari explorers, and says in his great work[1] on that region that he had learnt from extensive experience to be very careful in differing from any observation or statement of fact made by Livingstone. Of very few travellers can the same be said. All Livingstone's books are full of observations on anthropology, natural history, geography, and geology, which add greatly to their value and interest and give him a place apart among those African explorers who were not, like Schweinfurth and others, scientific specialists. Even towards the end, when he was racked with disease and suffering almost unbearable torture from dysentery as well as downright starvation, we find him noting down meticulously in his diaries the many curious scientific observations which he continued to make.

[1] Das Kalahari, 1904.

With this endowment and equipment, with a great liking for the wilds and the natives, and a passion for opening up the continent to civilization, he set forth in 1849 on his great adventure. With Oswell and Murray he reached Lake Ngami in the heart of the Kalahari that year; and in 1851, accompanied by his wife and children and Oswell, he reached the Zambesi at Sesheke—some forty miles above the Falls which, however, he did not see till four years later. The dangers of malaria, which he now first began to realize, and a sense of the magnitude of the task which lay before him, made him now take his family back to Cape Town and dispatch them to England. In June 1852 he was again on the Zambesi, and proceeded to explore the intricate river systems of the Zambesi and the Kwando rivers with their ramified connexions. The whole region is so flat that in the rainy season one can go backwards and forwards from one river to the other by innumerable channels, and the direction of the flow depends on the locality where the rain happens to fall, so that there is the confusing appearance of the water flowing in one direction at one time and in the opposite direction at another. He then moved on, tracing the upper course of the Zambesi to near its source, and then, having passed from the Zambesi to the Congo basin, he travelled westwards across Angola, crossed the Kasai river and other considerable tributaries of the Congo, and arrived at St. Paul de Loando in 1854, after incredible exertions and hardships, and looking on arrival more like a ghost than a human being. After recuperating here among the hospitable Portuguese, he returned with his small band of faithful Makololo to the Zambesi, where in the following year he reached the great Falls which he called after the name of Queen Victoria. Then turning north-west, he discovered the Kafue river, and following it arrived once more on the Zambesi; thus after the gravest dangers among warring native tribes he reached the Portuguese fort at Tete, and proceeded down the Zambesi to a point near its mouth. From here he went by land to Quelimane on the coast, having traversed the whole of southern tropical Africa from the Atlantic to the Indian Ocean, and being the first white man known to have done so. It was an enormous achievement, great from whatever point of view we look at it, but perhaps greatest in its effect on the public opinion of the world. Livingstone not only awakened Africa, but he did even more to awaken Europe and America to the possibilities of discovery in this mysterious continent. And from now onward we find a new era of African exploration opening, and all the most noted travellers hurrying on to attack the problems of the interior of Africa.

Livingstone's original object in this exploration of the Zambesi was to open up new communications to the interior of Africa. He had, to his surprise, learnt that here was not a desert as had been supposed, but a huge fertile portion of the earth with a high rainfall, great rivers, and high, healthy plateaux, which would present magnificent opportunities for commerce and development generally. The communications from the Cape were, however, too long and too difficult through the arid regions which had to be crossed in the south, and it was desirable to discover and develop the new lines of approach. The Zambesi struck him as the obvious new line of communication from the east coast, and seemed to be the solution of the commercial problem with which he had set out.

But this trek across Africa had opened his eyes to a fresh problem, one which especially struck deep chords in his humanitarian soul. On the Zambesi, and more so as he travelled farther north through Angola, he came across the ravages of the slave trade. His missionary instinct fastened at once on to this terrible situation which confronted him, and from now on it was difficult to say whether his passion for geographical discovery and commerce or his intense desire for the suppression of the slave trade was his strongest impelling motive. Henceforth he became the most active and powerful opponent of the African slave trade; and his continuous and unremitting propaganda against it was the main factor in its ultimate undoing. When in the near future the great monument arises near the Falls, it will commemorate not only the supreme African explorer, but also the heroic liberator of Africa from its oldest scourge, the curse which has probably caused more bloodshed and suffering on that continent than any other in all its history. Livingstone did not live to see the fruit of his labours, and the last years of his life were spent, in the region of the Lualaba river and in Tanganyika, amid the horrors of this curse and its fierce expiring convulsions. But if the question had been put to him whether he would rather be the great African explorer or its liberator from the slave trade, he would unhesitatingly have chosen the latter. Fate has willed that he should be both: and it would be difficult to conceive higher double honours for any man. To Livingstone there did not come the happy consciousness of success, but too often the sense of failure, of labouring against impossible odds. What was worse, he soon realized to his horror that he was unwittingly a potent means of facilitating the slave trade. For he discovered routes which the slave-traders had not ventured to open up themselves, but which they were only too eager to follow up in his wake. His name and character proved not only a passport for himself, but also for the enemies of his work, who followed after him; and it was a tragedy that the slave trade extended its terrible ravages on a large scale, both on the Zambesi and in the area of the Lakes, as a direct result of his discoveries. But in spite of appearances the end was near, and within a little more than a decade of Livingstone's death the slave trade had been practically exterminated by the Powers on the African continent. It is sad to think that its last refuge is with the only independent native states in Africa, and one can only hope that the League of Nations, of which those States are members, will not tolerate this situation much longer.

To return now to our narrative of discovery. The wonderful achievement of Livingstone had opened the floodgates of African adventure. Burton and

Speke, who had already explored Somaliland in 1854, were in 1856 sent by the Royal Geographical Society of London to discover and explore the great lakes, of which Krapf and Rebmann had brought rumours from Mombasa. The journey proved epoch-making; they reached Lake Tanganyika and explored its northern half, and Speke then pushed on to the southern shore of Victoria Nyanza. Hurrying back to England while Burton was still struck down with illness, Speke induced the Royal Geographical Society to send him once more to the lake which he had discovered. With Grant he reached the southern gulf of Victoria Nyanza, which bears his name. Thence they proceeded northwards, struck the Nile, where they were met and relieved by Sir Samuel Baker, and returned by the Nile to Egypt. It was a marvellous journey, but in the course of it they had curiously missed the Albert Nyanza. Sir Samuel Baker and his wife were at that time busy exploring the Upper Nile, after having explored Abyssinia and the Abyssinian tributaries of the Nile. They (the Bakers) then proceeded south, and reached the Nile in the Nyoro country, where they were detained and suffered the most terrible hardships. They also discovered Albert Nyanza and saw both the entrance and the exit of the Nile into and out of this lake. They then returned north to Gondokoro and followed the route of the Nile back to Egypt in 1865, after having completed one of the most arduous pieces of African exploration.

Meanwhile in 1859 Livingstone, now appointed

British Consul with government equipment and accompanied by another Scotsman, Dr., afterwards Sir,
John Kirk, had returned to the Zambesi, and was
experimenting on its suitability for steam navigation
with a view to opening up easier communications
with the interior. The main, and indeed insuperable,
obstacle proved to be the Kibebrassa rapids which he
had encountered on his previous journey. He repeatedly sailed up and explored the Shiré river, which
is the biggest northern affluent of the Zambesi, and
here, too, encountered rapids, which he called after
Sir R. Murchison. To the east of the Shiré he discovered Lake Shirwa in most beautiful country among
the high Milanje mountains; and in a subsequent trek
reached and discovered Lake Nyassa itself in September 1860. This lake and the surrounding country
made such an impression on Livingstone that he
thought the route of the lake would become the key to
South-central Africa. His views on the Zambesi route
were, however, undergoing a change. The rapids of
the Shiré, the troubles of the slave trade, and the un-
favourable attitude of the Portuguese induced him to
look for an alternative route to the lake. After a rapid
visit up the Zambesi to the Falls and Sesheke to re-
patriate his faithful Makololo following, he returned to
the mouth of the Zambesi, and there found the Universities' Mission which had come to Nyassa on his
appeal. Before locating it on the lake, he proceeded
to explore the route of the Rovuma river, which lies
just to the north of the Portuguese territory, and
which he imagined rose from the high country north

of the lake, and outside of Portuguese territory. Should this Rovuma route prove practicable for navigation, his intention was to locate the mission accordingly, to cut out the Portuguese and to adopt the Rovuma instead of the Zambesi as the route to the interior. His exploration of the Rovuma convinced him that this was not possible; the river was not navigable for any considerable distance, and it rose in the high country to the south-east of the lake. He then proceeded to settle the mission on the Shiré; but it subsequently failed and had to be abandoned because of the ravages and chaos created by the slave trade. In the meantime Livingstone and Kirk had gone forward to explore Lake Nyassa more fully; they covered the whole length of the lake (September–November, 1861), found the slave trade worse at its northern end, and returned to the Zambesi, where his wife was awaiting him. His joy was shortlived; first came the news of the death of Bishop Mackenzie and the failure of the Nyassa mission, and a little later Mrs. Livingstone sickened of malaria and died (27th April 1862). This heroic daughter of the Moffat family was fittingly buried under an enormous baobab tree at Shupanga on the Zambesi. The family has continued to play a great part in South Africa, and one member is now Prime Minister of Rhodesia. On a renewed visit up the Shiré Livingstone found the country desolated by the slave trade. He became convinced that there was nothing further to be done there, and he felt relieved when shortly afterwards his expedition was, probably at the instance of

Portugal, recalled by the British Government. Before leaving he made one more exploring tour, this time towards the west of Lake Nyassa, with the intention of reaching a big lake to the far north-west of which he had heard. This lake (Bangweolo) he did not reach on this occasion, but he discovered it five years later, and there, ultimately, the end came of all his Herculean labours.

In 1866 Livingstone, now out of the government as well as the mission service, and therefore entirely on his own very slender resources, resumed the project of reaching this mysterious Lake Bangweolo. He travelled south-westwards from the Rovuma river, then turned north-west from the southern end of Lake Nyassa, and proceeded to the southern end of Lake Tanganyika, from where he went first west and then south to discover the mighty Luapula river and Lakes Moero and Bangweolo in 1868. From there he returned to Tanganyika, and in the depth of his poverty was reduced to travelling in the train of some friendly slave dealers. He travelled westward to the Manyema country and reached Nyangwe on the Lualaba, which was probably the centre and depot of the slave trade, and where he saw the most heartrending sights of its ravages. He was at this time preoccupied with the problem of the ultimate sources of the Nile, and was trying to find out whether the Lualaba was the beginning of the Nile or of the Congo. Its northerly course, which he was told continued for a very long distance, pointed to its connexion with the Nile; but there was also the rumour that it finally turned west, and this again pointed to a Congo connexion. To solve this problem he might have to go farther north to the Nile or to the west coast. Before proceeding with his investigations, he was compelled by poverty to return to Tanganyika, and there at Ujiji he was in 1872 found and relieved by H. M. Stanley, who had been sent on a relief expedition by the *New York Herald*. Stanley returned after re-equipping Livingstone for his further march, and in August 1872 the veteran was once more on the move. Instead of proceeding to the north to follow the course of the Lualaba river, as one would expect, he turned south in order first to test a story in Herodotus to the effect that the ultimate source of the Nile is one of two conical hills in Central Africa, which Livingstone identified with two hills to the west of Lake Bangweolo. From this point he then intended, after visiting the ancient copper mines at Katanga, to turn north and test this story as well as the true relationship of the Lualaba. It was a wonderful undertaking for a man of sixty, with a frame already worn out by excessive labours and suffering from a most exhausting form of chronic dysentery. But there burnt in him a light of the spirit which nothing could quench. The whole of this march for the next eight months was one long agony. In November a severe rainy season set in which laid the country through which he was marching under water; food was scarce, often unobtainable, and the whole party was continually suffering from starvation. The dysentery became worse with the rough fare, and Livingstone was so weak that he had often to be carried. In January 1873 he was once more in the region of Lake Bangweolo. His condition was pitiable and the plight of his party desperate. Still he struggled on with indomitable courage. It is impossible to read his journals at this time without deep emotion. Although often scarcely conscious he continued to push on; the men waded through a country which resembled a lake; while he was carried in a fainting condition and suffered the intensest agony, on the shoulders of his faithful Susi or Chumo. The last entry on 27th April reads: 'Knocked up quite, and remain—recover—sent to buy milch goats.' This was at Chitambo s village, Ilala, to the south of Lake Bangweolo. There the end came in the early morning of 1st May 1873. His dead body was found kneeling in prayer. His heart was buried there by his devoted followers. His name and work will live for ever. Apparently down and out, he had achieved and left a work whose results were secure beyond all failure. While his body was being carried to the coast it was met by Lt. Lovett Cameron, who had been sent on a relief expedition by the Royal Geographical Society of London. Cameron rightly decided to push on, crossed Tanganyika and the Lualaba, then turned south-west through the somewhat advanced country of the chief Mwata Yanvo in Portuguese Angola, and finally arrived at Benguella in November 1875, after one of the historic marches across Africa. In an account of African exploration I was surprised to find the statement that Lovett Cameron was 'the first

Englishman to cross Africa'. This appears to be a fact in spite of his suspiciously Scotch name.

To go back for a moment: In the sixties three German travellers explored northern Africa—Dr. Rohlfs the western Sahara and the regions south of it to the Gulf of Guinea; Dr. Nachtigal the eastern Sahara and the regions to the south of it, including Lake Chad, Bagirmi, Wadai, and Kordofan; Dr. Schweinfurth, the Upper Nile and Nubia, the Bahr el Ghazal, and the Monbuttoo country in the Welle watershed of the Congo. I have not time to refer in detail to their explorations. They rank among the greatest of African travellers and were examples of a new type of explorer, whose object was science rather than merely geographical discovery. They have left wonderful accounts of their work. Thus the famous botanist Schweinfurth's book called *The Heart of Africa* is probably one of the most fascinating accounts of African travel ever written. His description in it of the capital and court of King Munza of the Monbuttoo cannibals is a rare masterpiece.

The same year that Cameron completed his journey across Africa, Stanley, once more at the instance of some enterprising newspapers, entered the lists of African discovery and soon solved the problem of the Lualaba river, which had troubled Livingstone to the last. Moving from the East coast in 1875 he proceeded to the Lakes, circumnavigated both Victoria Nyanza and Tanganyika, then marched on to the Lualaba, took to his boats and stuck to the river resolutely in spite of the most enormous difficulties, finally proving it to be the Upper Congo by emerging by the Congo on the Atlantic. Great as were the results of his expedition, they were surpassed by his epoch-making journey twelve years later for the relief of Emin Pasha in the Equatorial Sudan after the Mahdi revolt, the death of Gordon, and the fall of Khartoum. Starting up the Congo, Stanley proceeded to the junction of the Aruwimi river, and at that point entered the unknown, almost impenetrable African rain forest, through which he kept cutting his way for the next five months. He encountered incredible difficulties, but finally succeeded in reaching Albert Nyanza, relieved Emin and took him and his companions to the East coast, discovering en route Mount Ruwenzori, or the Mountains of the Moon, Lake Albert Edward, and the Semliki river flowing from it into Albert Nyanza, and thus tracing the westernmost sources of the Nile. His experiences in the forest and his minor discoveries on this great expedition were also of intense interest. Indeed nothing so striking had been seen in African travel, and the fate of his rearguard combined with the success of his vanguard to make this closing expedition the most spectacular in all African explorations.

The fates of Livingstone and Stanley are curiously linked in the story of African exploration, and it was Stanley's lot to complete the work of Livingstone in respect both of discovery and the suppression of the slave trade. In fame too, they stand out above all other African travellers. In actual geographical results the work of Stanley probably ranks first of all

African discoverers. And if on the whole I feel inclined to award the palm to Livingstone, it is because
he was the first, the pioneer of African discovery, and
because he achieved his colossal results single-handed,
with no material equipment, and, as it were, by sheer
moral force. The expeditions of Stanley were
equipped on a lavish scale, and resembled and were
carried on mostly like military expeditions. The two
men were so different that it is difficult even to compare them, but I should say that in Livingstone's
place and with the equipment with which Livingstone achieved his marvellous results, Stanley would
in all probability have done worse.

The world-wide impression and interest caused by
the tragic death of Livingstone in the swamps of
Lake Bangweolo, the return of the Cameron expedition, and the subsequent spectacular success of the
first Congo exploration of Stanley combined to lead
to a new situation in Africa. King Leopold of the
Belgians was the first in the field with an international African Congress at Brussels, which added
to the growing excitement. African exploration was
rapidly leading to a new phase which was of a
political character. In fact the train was being laid
for that scramble for Africa, which was to result a few
years afterwards in the partition of Africa among the
Powers. It soon became clear that King Leopold was
not acting merely in the general interests of science
and philanthropy, but of Belgium. Germany and
France were not slow to follow suit, and African
exploration was fast becoming a political game for

staking out national claims in Africa. There was a sudden and almost romantic revival in the suppression of the slave trade. Where the British Navy had hitherto borne the burden almost single-handed, active interest began suddenly to be displayed by the European Powers. The suppression of the slave trade became a convenient cloak for territorial ambitions and annexations. Thus evil often takes a hand in furthering good. The annexationist ambitions of States combined with the high humanitarian efforts of Livingstone to lead to a rapid decline of this oldest and most nefarious scourge of the continent. The partition of Africa took a new turn in 1884; in the following year the Berlin Conference prohibited the slave trade and the supply of fire-arms to the natives of Africa. By the end of the eighties and the beginning of the nineties the Arabic slave power had collapsed and the slave chiefs were in flight from the continent. At Nyangwe on the Lualaba, where Livingstone had been forced to witness the most revolting slave outrages, their last stand was made and their power was finally broken. Such is the irony of history.

Besides the names I have mentioned, there is a long and honourable roll of African exploration. I have but touched on the most salient facts and features and events, and I now pass on to consider some of the humanitarian, political, and economic results of all these vast labours, which have led, or rather one hopes may eventually lead, to the redemption of Africa.

The partition of Africa, which had commenced

with the scramble of 1884, was completed in the nineties; and as a result practically the whole of Africa, with the exception of Abyssinia, passed under white control. Portugal remained with her old African colonies, but with their area extended from the neighbourhood of the West and the East coasts far into the interior. Belgium, through the astuteness of King Leopold, had carved out the choicest slice of the continent, to which in the nineties was added the most valuable area of all, namely the Katanga. France, Germany, and Great Britain each staked out large and valuable territories and placed them under protected chartered companies. The marvellous romantic era of exploration was followed by a period of intensive exploitation. It became clear to the world that the key to the future was held largely by the tropics, that tropical products were not only essential industrial requirements of a highly developed civilization, but also promised to be equally valuable instruments of world power. Cotton, sisal, rubber, vegetable oils and fats, and the like, were the foundations not only of industrial, but also of world power. Millions of pounds were rapidly poured into the new territories and development was forced in every direction. Colonial expansion became a cardinal item in the programme of some at least of the Powers. It found forcible expression in the clamour for a place in the sun, which helped to produce the mentality that led to the Great War. Africa, which to Livingstone had been a high spiritual quest, and to other discoverers an adventure of unsurpassed romance, had finally become one of the apples of discord between the Powers. The Morocco policy of France led to compensations to Germany in the Congo basin. Secret treaties which meant a repartition of large parts of Africa were projected. And then the Great War came, the existing arrangements were thrown into the melting-pot, and Africa once more entered upon a new phase in her history of surprises.

The tramp of big armies was once more heard on this continent. Where Livingstone had marched with his tens, where Stanley had marched with his hundreds, the military commanders marched with their tens of thousands. My advance in the German East campaign often followed for long distances the routes of the great travellers whose exploits I have recounted. As a boy I had read their books with burning interest and intense longing to see those wonderful countries. And when at last my opportunity came, it was under circumstances such as no one could ever have foreseen in the wildest of dreams. The result of the War, so far as Africa was concerned, was a repartition under the Mandate system, which I had suggested as both a check and an advance on the old policy of colonial annexation. Germany lost her array of African colonies and they went under mandates to France, to some members of the British Empire, and in a lesser degree to Belgium.

But to Africa the War meant something far more serious than a fresh partition. Instead of the old pre-war collaboration of Europe, which existed even in spite of rivalries, Africa saw the European front, the front of European culture, broken, the European Powers at war with each other, and the natives of Africa enlisted in a great war between the whites. The black manhood of Africa was involved in the war, either as combatants or as porters and carriers. They shared in and endured all the hardships of the African campaigns, and the rude awakening has opened an entirely new chapter in the history of Africa. Africa has at last been roused from her historic slumbers. The peoples of Africa are infected with the vague unrest which has universally followed the Great War. For better or worse the old Africa is gone and the white races must face the new situation which they have themselves created in this continent. Africa is going to be one of the major problems of the twentieth century, and the repercussions of that problem on the rest of the world may be very far-reaching yet. How far the African natives will be able to go in the march on which they have started, what equilibrium will be reached eventually between their traditional system and the more complex features of European civilization, no one can foretell. Nor am I going to discuss these questions here to-night. Some aspects of the great African problem I am discussing in my lectures at Oxford. Here I only mention the fact that we are confronted with a new situation all over Africa, partly as a result of the experiences through which the natives passed in the Great War, and partly as the result of the rapidity with which almost revolutionary changes have supervened on the old order in Africa.

The question of transport and communications for the interior greatly preoccupied Livingstone as we have seen. His favourite idea of developing the Zambesi for transport to the interior has been abandoned, and, indeed, was abandoned by himself. But other great rivers—the Congo, and the Niger, in addition to the Nile—are to-day among the principal means of communication on the continent. Railway communications have been opened up on a large scale. With the exception of two short breaks, one between Victoria and Albert Nyanza, and the other beyond Albert Nyanza to Rejaf, it is to-day possible to pass uninterruptedly by rail and river steamer from Capetown to Alexandria. From the East coast, railway lines pierce the interior, not only in the Union of South Africa, but in Rhodesia, in Tanganyika, in Kenya, and from the Red Sea in Egypt and Abyssinia. From the West coast, railway lines cut into the interior in South-west Africa, in Angola, in Nigeria, in Sierra Leone, in Senegal, and other parts of North-west Africa. Next year the Lobito Bay railway will reach the Katanga copper-mines, while another from Bukama to Luebo (or Francqui) already connects these important mines with the navigable Kasai in the Congo basin, thus giving continuous railway communication for 3,300 miles from Cape Town to Francqui. Most ambitious of all, a railway has been projected to connect within the next decade the French territories on the Mediterranean across the Sahara with Timbuktu on the Niger. Motor transport is already beginning to re-

place camel transport along this route. Motor transport moves freely across the sandy Kalahari, along
routes which were impossible for the ox-wagon in
Livingstone's time. A so-called all-weather motor-
road exists between South Africa and the British
colonies under the Equator. To-day one can move
easily and freely across Africa in a comparatively
short time, whereas a generation ago the venture-
some traveller organized elaborate safaris, took years
and incurred grave difficulties and dangers in crossing
the continent, and became famous when successful.
Movement in almost all directions across the continent is becoming usual, and is breaking down very
rapidly what remains of the old tribal divisions and
partitions on the continent. The effect of all this on
African development and on native mentality can be
imagined.

Another potent factor for change and progress is
mining in Southern Africa. The southern portion of
the continent is exceptionally rich in minerals and has
been a mining area from time immemorial, so much
so that prospecting in Southern Africa often means
looking for ancient disused mines. Through mining
it is therefore susceptible of very rapid development.
There is no doubt that mining is the most effective
means of rapid development in a new country. A
large mining and trading population is attracted, and
local markets are developed which again call for a
farming population. In the following lecture I shall
stress the importance of diamond and gold mining
in the development of the old Cape Colony and the

Transvaal. But for the discovery of rich mines the history of South Africa would have been very different from what it has been during the last half-century. Now in the heart of Southern Africa immense copper-fields have been discovered and are being opened up in the Katanga and Northern Rhodesia. In the countries where the lonely Livingstone wandered, not far from the lake where he died, a vast network of mines is arising, the effect of which on the future of African development must be immense. Engineers calculate that in Northern Rhodesia alone ten million tons of ore will be treated annually within the next ten years, with a probable annual yield of 250,000 tons of copper, which eventually may be doubled. The Katanga copper mines just across the border already produce over 100,000 tons of copper per annum, and big extensions are contemplated. This will mean a large white mining population in the heart of Africa, and this again will bring about agricultural settlement on a large scale on the fertile highlands of Eastern Africa. A great labour force will have to be recruited from the Congo, Northern Rhodesia, Angola, and Nyassaland to do the rough mining work. What the Witwatersrand has meant farther south, that this copper-field may come to mean for the development of South-central Africa. It is therefore not difficult to appreciate that great changes are coming and that the old order in Southern Africa is definitely going. The new situation will present difficult social and political problems of the contact between European civilization and native culture, which will tax the statesmanship of this and the coming generations to the full. There will be no infallible rule or code to follow. We shall have to be guided by experience; we shall have to hammer out solutions as we go along. Let those who watch our experiments from afar bear in mind that in Africa we are facing the most perplexing racial situation which has ever been faced in the world. We can no longer follow the path of repression which formerly would have commended itself wherever a superior culture came in contact with a lower, more primitive. We cannot mix the two races, for that means debasement of the higher race and culture.

The future in Africa is to those peoples who, like the British and the Dutch, have steadfastly endeavoured to be loyal to their racial and cultural ideals as a European community. But if the extremes of repression and miscegenation are both excluded, we are left with a problem in racial contact between advanced Europeans and primitive Africans which is not only novel, but also most complex, and in which no guidance can be derived from the past experience of the world. The superior Aryans, when they settled in India among a lower, more primitive indigenous population, built up an elaborate caste system for their own racial and cultural protection. But the Indian caste system would not be possible under modern conditions, and in any case it would be a system impossible for Europeans with their ideals of life. Europeans in Africa who mean to be faithful to themselves and their traditions therefore have to face a situation, as novel and difficult as any that has ever confronted mankind. Africa will indeed apply the severest possible test to our European system with its ethical Christian ideals. I wish you to appreciate the magnitude of the task on which we are engaged in Africa. A grand experiment in racial and cultural contacts is being tried and tested out, which is fraught with enormous issues for the future of our civilization. If black and white in Africa, while faithful to themselves, can manage to evolve a plan according to which they can jointly develop the resources of this continent, a great service will be rendered for the future of the human race.

I have stressed the mining development in Southern Africa; an even more important agricultural advance is being made farther north throughout Central Africa. The external trade of British West Africa alone amounts to about £60 million per annum, and that of British East Africa from Uganda to Northern Rhodesia amounts to something under £30 million. These figures show what an advance has already been made in the short number of years since these territories settled down under white rule. In countries where practically no foreign trade existed a generation ago, where chiefs and people alike begged for hongo from passing travellers and explorers, where beads and the like represented the medium of exchange, we have to-day settled communities with great productive power, and with organized governments which they maintain. The figures I have just

mentioned refer only to the British possessions, and
the total for Africa, apart from South Africa and the
Mediterranean countries, is very much larger. Yet in
Livingstone's day they were mostly *terra incognita*,
with a trade which was practically negligible apart
from slavery.

People in this country have little conception of the
great development which has already taken place in
British Africa in little more than one generation, or
of the greater developments that are ahead. It is
probable that in another generation British Africa
may, with wise handling and proper stimulus, become as important a factor for British trade as India
itself. There will be immense tropical production,
and there will be a corresponding market for manufactures. Both from a humanitarian and a commercial point of view Africa deserves the close attention
and steady encouragement of the Governments concerned.

I have mentioned the set-back to the Universities'
Mission at Nyassa in the sixties. The failure was
only apparent and was shortlived. The mission, in
which Livingstone was so deeply interested, was
almost immediately restarted from Zanzibar as its
base, and it has within the last half century achieved
an outstanding record of success. Its example has
been followed by many other missionary bodies in
all parts of Africa. It is difficult to conceive what
Africa would have been without the civilizing effects
of the Christian missions. Mistakes have been made.
But the magnitude of the real service is out of all

comparison to those incidental mistakes. Missionary
enterprise, with its universal Christian message, and
its vast educative and civilizing effort, is and remains
the greatest and most powerful influence for good
in Africa.

The missionary, the trader, the traveller, the rail-
road builder, the labour recruiter, and the soldier
have wrought vast changes in Africa since Livingstone's day. He was the first, the greatest, and the
most beneficent of the new forces for change and progress. Africa is to-day on the move in all directions
and its ancient quietude is profoundly disturbed.
Yet one hopes that whatever developments may be in
store for it, it will preserve some of the old characteristics which have constituted its perennial charm in
the past. As long as Africans remain Africans, the
happy song and the dance will continue to brighten
the villages of Africa; that wonderful wild music,
with instruments wilder still, will continue to make its
peculiar appeal. The children of nature will continue
to enjoy the simple joys of village life, and in their
sunshine the gloom and the stern temper of colder
Europe will never prevail. Sensuous paganism will
always temper the ethical imperative, and religion
even at its best will still be of the earth, earthy. And
beyond the human inhabitants there will remain, one
hopes for centuries to come, the wild animals which
make this continent so attractive to the lover of
nature. I look forward to the time when the rage for
destruction will have disappeared, when the senseless
slaughter of the wild fauna will be as criminal and

contrary to public opinion as cruelty to humans, and when those who love the wilds and their shy denizens and intimate ways will come from all parts of the earth to find peace and refreshment in Africa. In the stress and strain of civilization, the nervous tension of high culture and the friction of our industrial system, Africa will be a place of refuge, a temple set apart where the human spirit can once more practise nature worship, and enjoy peace and quietude.

Africa in spite of all change will still remain Africa, and its most distinctive features among the continents will continue to be its untamed wildness, its aloofness and solitude, and its mysterious, eerie, brooding spirit.

II
AFRICAN SETTLEMENT

AFRICAN SETTLEMENT

I AM deeply sensible of the honour which Oxford University and the Rhodes Trustees have done me by inviting me to deliver the Rhodes Memorial Lectures. A previous invitation I had felt bound to decline, on the plea of pressing public duty. But when, after my recent defeat in the South African elections, the invitation was kindly renewed, I was left with no plausible excuse for not accepting the embarrassing honour. And so here I am to-day, a working politician, strange to your academic world, facing an audience accustomed to a very different bill of fare from that which I am able to place before you. My distinguished predecessors in this lecture-ship make my position even more unenviable. Sir Robert Borden was an Elder Statesman of the Empire who could discuss with expert skill its recent transformations in which he had played a leading part. His leisure and retirement from politics made him almost an Olympian in the realm of constitution-making on which he addressed you. He was followed by two famous scholars who could speak to you from an abundance of leisured study and meditation. How different is my position! I come to you with the marks of the battle and the dust of the fray still fresh upon me, with little opportunity for preparation, and with no experience at all in handling academic audiences. I pray for your kind indulgence. Remember the case of Rhodes, who, though not a lecturer himself, was in this Foundation the maker of lecturers. He was not a scholar, he had no leisure or inclination for academic pursuits; his haunts were the highways of the world. And yet you have accepted him as one of the Founders. He was a politician in active practice, a financier up to all the tricks of the trade, a man of the world, far away from the world of scholarship. But he had a priceless faculty of imagination, of vision, of seeing the greater plan into which the details of his working life and his daily task fitted. And so from mere politics and finance he evolved the larger policies, he drew the inspiration of the larger visions, which will remain when his finance and his politics have been long forgotten. My qualification as a Rhodes lecturer is that I am, like him, an active politician, that like him I am an African whose life-work has lain in the same field of African policies as his lay.

On this ground I claim to have some right to speak to you on the larger policies for which Rhodes stood. Other lecturers may have to go far afield in search of suitable subjects for their discourse. I am going to speak to you on the ideas and policies with which Rhodes's name is for ever inseparably associated. Those ideas and policies have not grown old or stale with time; on the contrary, they are to-day more alive than ever before. It is ever the hall-mark of genius to initiate points of view which are not a flash in the pan, but burn with a steady brilliance, to launch ideas whose fruitfulness increases with time and which thus carry their own immortality. I was a young man fighting in the Boer War when Rhodes passed away twenty-seven years ago. My whole working life since then has been continuously occupied with the same sort of questions which governed his thought—the Union of South Africa, the progress of European civilization on the African continent, the relations between white and black in that civilization, the promotion of world peace through better understanding between the leading nations of the world. Of these questions one—the Union of South Africa— has been happily solved. The others are in process of solution, or still await solution, and are to-day more important than they were in Rhodes's time. I shall in these lectures deal with these questions of African settlement, Native Policy in Africa, and World Peace; and I begin to-day with African settlement.

How keen Rhodes was on the settlement of a European population in the undeveloped spaces to the north of Cape Colony and the Transvaal is shown by the tremendous efforts he made to acquire and settle Rhodesia. To this end he laboured and fought for years, he plotted and schemed, he spent his money like water, and he risked his reputation and his life. The original Charter for Rhodesia covered Nyassaland also, for the administration of which he willingly paid. And in the end he won through. The settlement of a growing prosperous white people within the tropics, which is now in its second generation, is proof that his instinct was right, and that his policy

of 'homes, more homes' on the veld was no mere
chimera. Southern and Northern Rhodesia, marching far north into the tropics, with a thriving population in ever-increasing numbers, has completely
justified his dream of a European State in tropical
Africa. But his vision and his work were not limited
to the Rhodesias. To him they were but the free
passage to the farther north, the open door for a
civilization from the south which would ultimately
link up with the lands of the Mediterranean. The
formula of 'Cape to Cairo' summed up in a phrase
this northern policy.

Let me pause for a moment to refer to a criticism
sometimes made of this settlement policy of Rhodes.
It has been said that settlement was not really his object. He occupied Rhodesia in order to possess and
work its mines and minerals. The declared settlement policy was only a blind to cover his real thirst
for minerals. This charge is but an echo of another
charge often levelled at Rhodes in his lifetime. But
it will not stand examination. Money-making never
was an end in itself to Rhodes, but always a means
to the attainment of his ends. Money literally was
the sinews of war to him. Whatever money he made
he spent most lavishly to prosecute the larger objectives he had in view. His trust deed for de Beers,
which made it possible to use the profits from the
Kimberley mines to finance the opening up of
Rhodesia, is conclusive proof of that fact. Rhodes
aimed both at the settlement of Rhodesia and at the
exploitation of its mineral resources. The one was

necessary to the other. Without mines to attract
whites, there would not be the settlers to settle nor
the means to settle them with. That was a lesson
which Rhodes had learnt from the history of South
Africa and other countries. The gold rushes to
California in the mid-nineteenth century had given
western America its great start and launched it on
its career of agricultural expansion. Similarly, the
diamond rush to Kimberley in the seventies and the
gold rush to Johannesburg in the eighties had revolutionized economic conditions in South Africa. Before
the first of these rushes the white population of
South Africa was 300,000. After the second of these
rushes at the end of the Boer War the white population had risen to 1,200,000. In one generation it had
quadrupled as a result of the discoveries of diamonds
and gold. Mining not only attracted people by itself;
it stimulated every other industry, and farming most
of all. It created a local market for the agricultural
and pastoral industries and thereby led to the rapid
settlement and effective exploitation of the land. In
Rhodesia, too, the mines have been the backbone of
the development and settlement of the country. One
is interested to see almost every town in that young
country settled on a mine. Rhodes was well aware
from his own experience that mining is the most
potent agency for the settlement of a country. He
therefore welcomed mining both for itself and for
what it led to in the way of general development.

It is not unreasonable to expect that mining will
continue to play a great part in the future settlement

and development of Africa. Southern Africa is
beyond doubt one of the most highly mineralized
areas of the world. Its gold mines have apparently
been worked from antiquity, and must in ancient
times have supported a very large population and a
much higher civilization than it has known up to our
own times. It has not only unique gold and diamond
deposits. It has enormous coal and iron deposits;
it has probably the largest copper deposits in the
world. And it contains in great abundance those base
minerals which are used for hardening iron and steel
and are therefore of the greatest industrial importance. The discovery and exploitation of these unique
resources will continue to attract and support a large
European as well as give employment to a far
larger native population. And the African countries
which have the most promising prospects from the
mineral point of view will outstrip the others in
population, in development, and in economic importance. The discovery of gold raised the Transvaal in one generation from the most backward
to the foremost state in South Africa. And the
same will happen again farther north. In the race
between the East African States the lead will probably soon be taken by Northern Rhodesia. This
Cinderella among African colonies is the lucky
possessor of enormous copper deposits, besides other
mineral resources which are only now beginning to
be scratched. It is not improbable that within the
next ten years Northern Rhodesia will have a mining
field second only to that of the Witwatersrand. What

that must mean for the development of Eastern Africa it is not easy to imagine. In the high lands of the Kafue and other areas there are also some of the richest and most valuable lands for agricultural settlement in all Africa. We should not be surprised to see in Northern Rhodesia another Transvaal on a smaller scale, with all that this will mean for the progress and civilization of this continent. A large European community settled on the healthy high lands in the heart of Africa, and forming not only a new centre but a fresh support and stimulus for Western civilization throughout vast surrounding areas, may well revolutionize the whole outlook for the future. It may give an opening for strengthening our civilization and reclaiming Africa from barbarism such as has never been dreamt of before. It is the very land where Livingstone toiled his hardest and perished gloriously in the end. What an act of historic justice it would be if this land becomes the centre of the great African Dominion which will realize his dream of civilization and commerce in Africa and revolutionize the position and prospects of civilization on this dark continent!

Rhodes's work for European settlement in Rhodesia did not stand alone. Circumstances seemed to favour his settlement policy farther north; the idea of European settlement throughout Eastern Africa seemed to find a ready response in high official quarters. The British Government invited and encouraged settlers to occupy British East Africa, and built the Uganda railway in order to facilitate this occupation. The German Government further south copied this example, and proceeded to settle a white population in the Usambaras and on the slopes of Kilimanjaro and Meru Mountains and elsewhere. To all appearance, the settlement of a white population on the high lands of Eastern Africa seemed not only to be the Rhodes policy, but also the British and the German policy. More recently still, after the conclusion of the Great War, the British Government proceeded to establish soldier settlements on most favourable terms in Kenya, and apparently looked upon such settlements as a satisfactory way of dealing with one of the post-war problems on its hands. The ousting of German rule from Tanganyika, the consolidation of British rule from the borders of Abyssinia to the south of the continent seemed to present the opportunity for a strong forward movement in this policy of settling the high lands of Eastern Africa, which stretch in an unbroken belt, hundreds of miles broad, from Kenya to South Africa. In spite of this, however, there is at present a slackening of this policy. There is doubt and hesitation. There is a slowing down at the very time when there should be a determined move forward. What is the explanation of this recent development? There are several answers, and it is necessary for us to review the position once more and so see whether the policy of African settlement rests on a secure and defensible foundation.

The root cause of this change of attitude is entirely creditable. It is the humanitarian feeling which has been on the increase since the Great War, which sides with the under-dog, which produces the policy of Africa for the Africans—that is, for the natives; which holds that Africa is a black continent, the home of the negro and negroid peoples, and that it should remain such; that the whites have Europe and America as their present and future homes, and that, just as the whites do not dream of colonizing yellow Asia, so they are not justified in intruding into this natural and predestined home of the blacks and of an indigenous native culture. This view was forcibly expressed by Lord Olivier in 1919 when he declared that 'settlements in Africa produce (as they have done in all ages and all countries), first, slavery, predial or domestic; second, compulsory or indentured labour; third, the expropriation of natives from the land in order to compel them to work for wages on the estates; fourth, pressure on the natives to labour for wages through direct or indirect taxation—each of which has in turn given rise to reactions of the humanitarian conscience.'[1]

Now, the answer to this form of argument is that it condemns a policy which may be wise and sound in itself, by pointing to the excesses and abuses to which it leads. I do not deny that there have been these abuses and that they have to be guarded against. I am wholeheartedly opposed to each and all of the tendencies which Lord Olivier sets out, and, I believe, so are, probably, all fair-minded white settlers in Africa to-day. They are not the policy, but the blots and

[1] *Contemp. Review*, Jan. 1919.

excrescences on the policy. White settlement can proceed in Africa without, and is all the better for being without, the dubious aids of slavery or forced or indentured labour, or labour taxes, or other forms of labour compulsion. Our experience in South Africa has definitely established that these expedients to help out the white settler are not only unnecessary but positively harmful. Slavery has definitely passed away so far as the whites are concerned; compulsory or indentured labour was formerly in existence but is now universally condemned, except for public works in certain special cases. Depriving natives of their land or of the land which is reasonably required for their present or future needs should also be out of the question, and in this respect white settlement should not, and, as I shall just now show, need not, conflict in any shape or form with the rights or needs of the natives. With regard to taxes, a small tax in the form of a hut or capitation tax is universally imposed on the natives as their contribution to the maintenance of good government. As a general tax it is fair and approved of by all native administrators, nor is it resented by the natives whose customs prescribe a contribution to the requirements of their chiefs. But a special labour tax is not warranted and is unnecessary. It has been repeatedly tried in South Africa, notably by Mr. Rhodes in his celebrated Glen Grey Act, and has as often had to be abandoned. It takes the raw native some time to acquire the habit of going out to work for the white employer. But as his economic needs develop, and they develop fairly

rapidly, and as he learns the value of ready money, it
soon becomes habitual for him to spend part of his
time in white employment. South African experience
is decisive on this point. Even for those natives, for
instance, in the Transkeian Territories, who have
ample land for their own needs, it soon becomes
customary to go out to work for part of each year in
the mines or industries or the neighbouring agricultural districts. No inducement is necessary beyond
their ordinary growing economic needs. Employment in European industries or with European
settlers soon becomes the regular routine, and the
natives are quite satisfied and happy to fall into this
routine of part-time employment. By temperament
they have not much initiative, and if left to themselves and their own tribal routine they do not
respond very well to the stimulus for progress. They
are naturally happy-go-lucky, and are not oppressed
with the stirrings of that divine discontent which have
made the European the most unhappy but the most
progressive of all humans. They are easily satisfied
and a very little goes a long way with them. As
workers they are slow, unintelligent, and essentially
imitative. They have little foresight and display little
forethought. But these very characteristics make
them take readily to a routine which is settled for
them by a white employer. And if they are well
treated they respond with that good temper and that
slow honest toil which makes them so easy to work
with and so acceptable to the white employer. For
thousands of years they have been accustomed to

domination by their chiefs, and therefore they readily accept the firm handling, the lead, and the mastery of the white employer. It fits in with their character and their age-long training.

I may here add the valuable opinion of the Hilton Young Commission:

'It is advantageous to the native to learn habits of regular work and to gain practical experience of what can be achieved by advanced methods of agriculture. In certain conditions also natives may be able to get a larger economic return from employment under Europeans than by working on their own account. Moreover, in the early days of British administration in such countries as the Eastern and Central African dependencies, an influx of European settlers with capital may be of great assistance to the Government in starting a process of economic development for the natives. Without some external impetus at the beginning, there may be no escape from a vicious circle. For while, on the one hand, measures necessary to improve the standard of native agriculture, such as the provision of agricultural inspectors, issues of seed, &c., cannot be undertaken by the Government without revenue, on the other hand the necessary revenue may not be available until some improvement in agricultural production is brought about. The activities of the settlers who have sufficient capital to carry them through the early unproductive years may provide the necessary impetus at the start.' [1]

From all this it follows that the easiest, most natural and obvious way to civilize the African native is to give him decent white employment. White employment is his best school; the gospel of labour is the most salutary gospel for him. The civilization of

[1] i, p. 64.

the African continent will be a vain dream apart from white employment, without the leading hand of the settler and the employer, away from the continuous living contact with the actual example and the actual practice of European industry and agriculture. The civilization of Africa therefore calls for a definite policy, the policy of European settlement, the establishment of a white community inside Africa which will form the steel framework of the whole ambitious structure of African civilization. Without a large European population as a continuous support and guarantee of that civilization and as an ever-present practical example and stimulus for the natives, I fear that civilization will not go far and will not endure for long. From the native point of view, therefore, just as much as from the white or European point of view, nay, even more from the native point of view, the policy of African settlement is imperatively necessary.

I find in recent years a tendency to give primacy to the native point of view, to place native interests first in the scheme for African development. This appears to be the attitude of the British Government in East Africa, at any rate since 1923. This attitude again has largely influenced the view of the various commissions of inquiry which have studied these vexed questions since 1923. Beyond that again is the slogan 'Africa for the Africans'. The underlying assumption of this view is that there is an essential incompatibility between white and native interests, that the promotion of white settlement must necessarily or usually run counter to native rights and interests, and that this encroachment can only be prevented by calling a halt to the policy of white settlement. My point is that, apart from abuses and avoidable excrescences, there is no such inherent and inevitable clash of interests between the two. If Africa is to be civilized at all, if the heavy responsibility for African civilization is not to be weakly renounced and abandoned, the two will have to go together in carrying the great burden. The native needs the white man even more than the white man needs the native; both are indeed necessary for the due performance of the heavy task. As the Ormsby-Gore Commission of 1924 said: 'In order to be pro-native it is not necessary to be anti-white. To be in favour of white settlement in such portions of Africa as are climatically suitable for European homes, it is not necessary to be anti-native. East Africa can only progress economically and socially on the basis of full and complete co-operation between all races.'[1] The assumption of conflict and incompatibility is quite wrong. White settlement along proper economic lines and on proper ethical principles is what black Africa most needs to-day for its development and civilization. Granting in principle that native interests should rank first, I still submit that white settlement under proper safeguards remains the best means to give effect to that priority. For without large-scale permanent European settlement on this continent the African mass will not be moved, the sporadic attempts at civilization will pass, Africa

[1] Cmd. 2387, p. 22.

may relapse to her historic and prehistoric slumbers, and once more only mining holes and ruined forts may ultimately remain to bear testimony to future ages of what once was. We shall have a repetition of Zimbabwe, and not an enduring impression on and betterment of the peoples of this continent.

To my mind we shall make a great mistake if we analyse the factors which bear upon African progress and civilization and begin to assign separate and contrasted and competitive values to them. African progress is one whole organic problem and has to be viewed as such. It is not really a case of natives first or whites first, but of Africa first. Any policy which (without manifest injustice or unfairness to any particular section) promotes most effectively African development and civilization as a whole will at the same time be most in the interest of the natives as well as of the whites. That is good political philosophy as well as sound common sense. If white settlement in suitable and available climatic areas is, as I contend, the most effective and expeditious means of pushing forward the economic progress of this continent, it will prove to be also the best means of promoting native interests. In support of this argument I may quote once more from the Report of the Hilton Young Commission: 'It is quite certain, for example that nothing like the present development of the high lands of Kenya could have been achieved without the introduction of a vigorous community of European settlers. While this development has increased the wealth of the world it may at

the same time benefit the natives, since, on the best
European farms, the natives may receive, through
contact with their white masters, an education more
practical and more formative than anything that they
can be taught in the schools. Notwithstanding the
difficulties to which it gives rise, white settlement
provides a stimulus and example which may in the
long run promote and hasten the progress of the
natives.'

But white settlement is not the only way to bring
European influence to bear on native progress. I am
told that there is the missionary, and there is the
government civil servant who may supply the necessary guidance without creating the crop of awkward
problems which white settlement usually produces.
Allow me a few words in reply to this argument.
Much as I admire the heroic spirit and the achievement of missionary enterprise, much as I respect the
contribution which the various African civil services
are making, I have no hesitation in saying that neither
separately nor together are they competent to play
the decisive part which is here assigned to white
settlement. The Christian missionary has, after a
century of ceaseless effort, not yet succeeded in making any deep impression on Africa. Compared to the
enormous progress and still rapid spread of Mohammedanism, his success is not very striking. These
words may sound cold and unsympathetic from
one who believes that the message of Christianity is
and remains the greatest inspiration of the human
race. But we must face facts. Mohammedanism is

already in solid and uncontested possession of Africa
from the Mediterranean to the tenth parallel of north
latitude, and to the south of it is spreading more
rapidly than Christianity. As a creed Mohammedanism makes a very strong appeal to the native mind,
perhaps stronger than that of the highly ethical and
spiritual Christian religion. For these and other
reasons I should not think it fair to leave the fate of
European civilization to the missionary alone. Even
Livingstone did not think so. And the missionary
of the old type no longer responds to the needs of
Africa. For the African even less than for the European the teaching of the gospel is not enough. The
scientific and medical aspects of mission work are
steadily coming to the fore. I do not know whether
you have read the book of Professor Schweitzer,
The Edge of the Forest Primeval. It is a most
informative book, and it points the way to the
future trend of missionary work. The true ruler of
Africa to-day, as he has been for thousands of years
in the past, is the medicine man; and the only man
to fight him effectively is the scientific medicine man.
It is a matter for congratulation that our Christian
missions are more and more developing their medical
side. Medical mission is the mission for Africa. The
devils of Africa are witchcraft and disease, with
which only medical science can cope properly. You
get a true picture of African witchcraft from Paul
de Chaillu's book *Equatorial Africa*, which, although
written some seventy years ago, still remains one of
the most illuminating documents on native African

life. Christian missionaries will in future require a thorough anthropological training in addition to a general scientific medical equipment. But even so, and however well-trained and well-equipped they may be, the task of European civilization in Africa will need the weight and the numbers and the constant example of large white communities for its progress and success.

Then there is the civil servant, the native administrator in Africa. His contribution to African progress has been very great, and I have the deepest respect for the human spirit of service, the incorruptible justice, the patience and high efficiency which the African civil services have brought to the performance of their heavy task. And they can point to remarkable success. In West Africa, for instance, the success of the civil servant in guiding native agriculture has been most striking. But recent developments in West Africa and Uganda have not lasted long enough to justify any sure conclusions. Cocoa, palm-kernels, and cotton have indeed led to a phenomenal economic development. But the real test is still to come, when competition elsewhere, under up-to-date methods and with scientific equipment, may once more put the native producer out of court. Already the wasteful character of native production is beginning to be realized, and misgivings are beginning to be felt about the future. While paying our tribute to the native administrator, guiding the native producer in the wilds of Africa, we should be wise to suspend final

judgement for the present. Nor does experience elsewhere justify a childlike faith in the official guidance
or control of industry. An English farmer or manu-
facturer would be horrified if he were advised to put
his faith in Government officials. The enterprise
and private initiative, the free experimentation and
taking of risks, which are essential to economic and
industrial success, are remote from the official routine
of the civil servant. The training of the civil servant
is to play for safety, to follow his book and stick to his
regulations. With him the fear of the inspector and
the auditor is the beginning of wisdom. He is not a
safe guide in the uncharted sea of industry: in
Africa perhaps even less than in Europe.

I now pass on to mention another objection which
is widely urged against white settlement in the
African tropics. It is said that such settlement must
encroach on the land which is needed for the natives,
that the inevitable tendency would be to oust the
natives from their ancestral lands, to restrict them to
limited reserves, and to cramp their future expansion.
This objection to white settlement is perhaps the one
which is most generally entertained and most honestly
felt, and it is the one in which there is the least substance. In the remarks I am now going to make I shall
confine myself to Eastern Africa. West Africa is admittedly a different situation. It is already fairly
thickly populated; it is climatically very unsuitable
for white settlement, which in consequence has never
been tried there. It is at present making fair progress
without any but official assistance, and in the interior

the negro population is already largely dominated and controlled by a superior emigrant race of Hamitic race and Moslem creed. In Eastern Africa I also except from my argument the low-lying countries of Uganda and Zanzibar, which are well populated and have no large areas climatically suitable for white settlement. We are left then with Kenya, Tanganyika, Nyassaland, and Northern Rhodesia, all four of which lie on the broad backbone of Eastern Africa and contain an abundance of elevated lands above 4,000 ft. high, in addition to immensely larger areas of fertile lowlands and river valleys. These territories comprise about a million square miles with a population of about twelve million natives. These twelve millions are mostly confined to the low-level areas, and even there occupy only a comparatively small portion of the land. Northern Rhodesia, which is more than double the size of the British Isles, with a high rainfall and a fertile soil, with much of its territory between 4,000 and 5,000 ft. above sea-level, and with a pleasant climate, has little more than four natives to the square mile—perhaps the most promising territory of Eastern Africa practically unoccupied. (Compare this figure with 36·2 in Northern Nigeria or 223 in British India.) The point that strikes the traveller forcibly in these territories is the extreme sparseness of the population and the large vacant areas everywhere stretching in all directions. The natives congregate into settlements and villages and tribal areas, leaving most of the land vacant. Leaving the natives all the land which is occupied by them, or which may become reasonably necessary for any future expansion, there will still be left immense unapportioned unoccupied areas. On one point there cannot be the least doubt, and that is that even with an extensive reservation of the high lands for white settlement there will always be more than enough land for all native purposes. Lord Lugard, after reviewing the statistics of land and population in both East and West Africa, concludes with the following observation:

'In all except the few very densely populated districts it may be said that there is ample room for the legitimate needs of alien (European) enterprise and development. In those regions, whether in the East or in the West, where European settlement is not possible, the demand for land by non-natives is so limited, the area available is so large, and except in limited districts, the native population is so small that, whether the Government in theory owns the land or not, it is not likely in practice that the native cultivator will find any difficulty in obtaining all the land he needs.'[1]

This opinion ought to satisfy even those who are most solicitous for the interests of the natives. I shall make one more quotation which will show that the Governors of the East African territories, in conference assembled in 1926, were agreed that the sparse native population of East Africa not only leaves the opening for white settlement in the high lands, but also calls for such settlement, if the productive power of those possessions is to be developed to the utmost:

'East Africa (they say) has two remarkable features which

[1] *Dual Mandate*, p. 332.

differentiate it greatly from British West Africa and from most of the Empire's other tropical possessions. In the first place, the population is very sparse by comparison with the extent of the territory and its potentialities. In the second place, large areas are by reason of their altitude suited climatically for European colonization.

'It is generally admitted that European control in some form is necessary to the welfare and development of the African peoples. In no other way can peace be secured, improper exploitation prevented, and the country developed to anything like its full producing capacity. Where the population is sufficiently numerous, the development can be carried on under European administration and the produce marketed by European merchants. This is the natural course of affairs in West Africa. But in East Africa the population is not sufficient to secure development in the same manner; and if the whole country were to be handed over to a policy of native production alone under the guidance of European administration, it would have to be constituted an economic sanctuary so as to prevent the economic needs of the outside world from forcing some other form of development upon it. For these reasons East Africa has already been committed to what is known as the dual policy—that is, to a combination of non-native and native production.

'The broad contrast presented by natural conditions in different parts of East Africa is illustrated by the difference between Kenya and Uganda. In Uganda the population is sufficient for native production on a very large scale, and the climate is also unsuitable for European colonization. Uganda is, therefore, developing broadly on the same lines as West Africa. In the high lands of Kenya, on the other hand, the native population is totally insufficient and unfitted to develop the country. Its present scale of production would, therefore, have been impossible unless the railway had been built across the high lands and had brought in its train several thousand European colonists. The contrast presented by

population can be maintained in the tropics; the adults cannot work under tropical climatic conditions, and thus become entirely dependent on black labour, and in the end parasitical, while children cannot be properly reared and brought up to healthy maturity. Although the altitude mitigates the heat it is said to produce a tendency to nervous excitement and strain. How far this objection is valid it is difficult, if not impossible, to say with our present limited knowledge. A white community has now been living for almost a generation in the high lands of Kenya and other parts of East Africa. In Rhodesia and South-West Africa, which are well within the tropics, white communities have been permanently settled for the last thirty to thirty-five years; large families are reared, and the school-children appear strong and healthy, and no different from children in the Union farther south. In the Transvaal, where the Rand and much of the high veld lies at an altitude of 5,000 to 6,000 ft., a large white population has been living for the last forty years and more, without any detriment to their health or physical fitness as a community. It is a fact that tropical and sub-tropical parts of South Africa, which once were thought unhealthy, now carry a large white population without any harm to health. In other parts of the world whites live permanently in the tropics at more or less high altitudes. Australian experience in northern Queensland is entirely favourable to white settlement in the tropics. The Director of the Australian Institute of Tropical Medicine, in a valuable report called 'The White Man in the Tropics' (1925), makes the following statement:

'Australia has the unique distinction of having bred up during the last seventy years a large, resident, pure-blooded white population under tropical conditions. For a considerable time it has been more and more apparent that the question of the possibility of establishing the white man in tropical countries, possessing no large resident native population, is infinitely more largely a question of preventive medicine than a question of climate. Climatic adaptation is certainly essential and must be assisted by habits and the provision of environmental circumstances which are in conformity with conditions of climate and temperature. While the attention of the world has been directed with incredulity and amazement upon small colonies of Europeans striving to obtain a footing in Brazil and Peru, Rhodesia, German South-West Africa, and other localities, thousands of Australians have been living in identical latitudes unaware that by so doing they were controverting the old-established, generalized dictum that the white man cannot persist under tropical conditions.'

The human body is very adaptable, and Europeans to-day thrive over the world under conditions very different from those which reared them originally in temperate Europe. In these matters we have not the actual experience or statistics which would justify definite conclusions. But the settlement of the high lands of Eastern Africa must necessarily take generations to carry out fully, and there will be time enough to watch the effects of the policy on the health and physical character of the population, and to slow down or speed up the process in accordance with the experience gained. The experiment, so far as it has already progressed in Rhodesia and Kenya, seems to justify the speeding up of the policy, and no undue weight should be attached to this particular difficulty, although the results of the policy, from the health point of view, will have to be carefully watched. It is even possible that just as in the biological world new types are evolved in a new environment, so a new human type may in time arise under the unusual climatic conditions of Eastern Africa. The Transvaal Boer already seems to be evolving into a type very different from his Dutch Huguenot ancestors. The human laboratory of Africa may yet produce strange results, and time alone can show whether or not the experiment was worth while in the interests of humanity.

I have now dealt with some of the doubts and difficulties which have been raised against white settlement in Eastern Africa, and I conclude with the positive reasons favouring such a policy. The British Government are to-day in control of a vast portion of the African continent, and especially of that part which, as far as evidence goes, appears eminently suitable for European colonization. It cannot simply sit on these vast assets and adopt a policy of drift. It is a trustee for civilization; it must see that the best use is made of this huge undeveloped estate. And such a role especially befits the greatest colonizing power the world has ever seen. The resources of Eastern Africa must be developed and exploited in a manner worthy of the traditions of Great Britain. I have tried to show that the claims of the natives to civilization, no less than the claim of the world to the vigorous development of these valuable tropical lands, calls for a great colonizing effort on the part of Great Britain. The building up of a strong white community to hold and develop the healthy high lands which stretch from Rhodesia to Kenya would be a magnificent response to this call. Now that Great Britain holds these territories from north to south in one unbroken chain, she has an opportunity, greater even than Rhodes dreamt of, to carry out her historic mission and establish in the heart of the African continent and as a bulwark of its future civilization another great European community. To me it seems the next critical step in the evolution of our Commonwealth of Nations. These fragments of Crown colonies should be put in the way of becoming in time another important self-governing unit of the Empire. There are here the makings of something of far-reaching importance for Africa, for the Empire, and for the world. But a definite forward policy is wanted which will eventually lead to this consummation. The future only can show whether this new group will be linked with the Union in the south or whether it will follow lines of its own in a new northern constellation. What is urgently wanted is the settlement of a white population, able and competent to undertake the task of development, and finally to conquer and hold this continent for European civilization.

There is another aspect of this question which I am sure will not be lost sight of in these days. The question of Empire migration bulks very large to-day, and if I read the signs of the times aright, it will bulk still larger in the years to come. Vast sums have been rendered available by the British parliament in order to promote the migration of the surplus population of this country to the distant vacant spaces of the Empire. The first measure of the new Labour Government in its effort to grapple with unemployment was a bill for subsidizing colonial development. There is an urgent double call—for easing the pressure in the narrow, overcrowded space at home, and for increasing it in the vast undeveloped estate of the Empire abroad. Rhodes's policy of 'more homes' in the outer Empire is to-day more urgent and important than ever before. The time is more than ripe for a real forward policy of migration and land settlement in the Empire. There are great spaces to be filled up in the Dominions, and the mother country and the Dominions have an equal interest in the common task, which they should share financially. They have not yet really come to grips with it. But besides the Dominions there is Africa calling. On this continent Great Britain and the Empire have a more unique position than in any other portion of the globe. There is land enough and to spare for all present and future native requirements. Over and above that there is a large surplus of high land available for white settlers who will not merely be white planters. The occupation of these high lands by a settled European population will, in the years to come, take away an appreciable number of your home population, and will provide work for much larger numbers at home. By a vigorous policy of settlement on these high lands from south to north of Eastern Africa you will lay the foundations of a great future Dominion of the Empire. The cause of African civilization will be advanced more securely by such a policy than by any other that I can conceive. And thereby will be achieved a stable and permanent civilization which will give the native peoples of Africa that age-long contact with a higher order of things which the exceptionally slow movement of the native specially calls for. No flash in the pan of tropical exploitation will really help the cause of African civilization. It will be a slow, gradual schooling of peoples who have slumbered and stagnated since the dawn of time, and only an ever-present, settled, permanent European order can achieve that high end. The call of Africa for civilization, the call of the world for tropical products, and the call of these islands for migration and employment all combine to give very real force to the case which I am making here to-day. From all these points of view the time has come for a real major advance, and I hope we shall not have long to wait for it.

I conclude with two practical suggestions. My first concerns the carrying out of the policy I have advocated. It may have struck you that I have avoided any direct discussion of the valuable Report of the Hilton Young Commission on the organization of Eastern Africa. I may point out that the recommendations of that report deal with a temporary and limited situation, with the next step which the political and administrative structure in East Africa calls for. My theme has been a different one—not political or administrative machinery, but the ultimate objectives of our African policy. I am pleading not for temporary measures but for the only sort of foundation which will securely bear the weight of future African development and civilization. A large white population seems to be a *sine qua non*; and in the long run they, in concert with the natives, will settle their own political arrangements. There is only one point where my plea links on to the special recommendations of the Report. The Report recommends that the East African territories shall be formed into two groups, in each of which a High Commissioner shall represent the Secretary of State for Colonies, and control and direct certain common policies of the group concerned—such as native policy, customs, transport, defence, and research. To these I would add land settlement. If land settlement in Eastern Africa were decided upon as a major policy, and men of·vision and wide sympathy and energy were appointed to be High Commissioners, the picture which I have tried to sketch to-day will not be long in taking shape. If the instrument is adequate to the task, the results may be very far-reaching. Land settlement should, however, be a common concerted policy and should not be left to local idiosyncrasies. And along with native policy it should be the most important constructive task of the new High Commissioners.

In the second place I would suggest that the essential unity of our African problems should be recognized by instituting an Annual Conference for their discussion, to which all the British African States from Kenya to the Union of South Africa will send delegates. It is too much to ask the young and immature white communities in the north to bear the whole weight of the vast issues upon which they are now embarking, as well as to bear the brunt of continual differences with Downing Street. There is great experience in the south which ought to be rendered available for the north. For a century and more South Africa has laboured and suffered over the very problems which are beginning to agitate the young communities in the north. This experience should be helpful beyond the Union. Many mistakes made in the south will then be avoided in the north, many new mistakes threatening in the north will appear as such in the light of South African experience. Interest in and concern for native progress and welfare are steadily growing in the Union of South Africa, in spite of all appearances to the contrary. Annual conferences by the leaders throughout Eastern and South Africa will provide the necessary forum for shaping common policies. And as a result of such conferences, the British Government and the High Commissioners will have a more responsible and mature white opinion to reckon with and to guide them in their task. An informal East African conference already exists so far as the territories from Rhodesia northwards are concerned. The Union should join this conference, and its organization should be regularized so that more weight will attach to its discussions and recommendations. Nothing in the nature of a parliament or even of a General African Advisory Council is intended or is necessary. A common forum for exchanging ideas, for clarifying viewpoints, for self-education of the leaders, and for hammering out common policies embodied in resolutions is all that is wanted. By such means a healthy public opinion will be formed, and the pitfalls due to the narrower local outlook will be avoided in matters of far-reaching common significance. Such a conference with a permanent secretariat will meet all the present needs of the case, and it may become an institution which will yet exercise a most important and beneficent influence over future developments on this continent—a sort of African League of Nations, in fact, for the British States.

The address which I have given to-day on the policy of white settlement in Africa is incomplete without the address on native policy which I intend to deliver on the 16th November. The two will together sketch an integral African policy, the native and white aspects of which are closely interdependent.

III

NATIVE POLICY IN AFRICA

NATIVE POLICY IN AFRICA

OUR subject to-day will be African Native Policy. It bristles with difficult and contentious issues, and I must crave your attention to what may be a tedious discussion. If, owing to the short time at my disposal, I pass lightly over certain points, you must bear in mind that nevertheless I am fully aware of their importance. In our discussion of white settlement in Africa a good deal was said also on native policy, but only incidentally, as bearing on the subject of white settlement. But native policy deserves to be considered by itself, as it is far and away the most important issue which is raised by our European contact with the African continent and its peoples. The policy or policies which the European peoples are going to pursue towards the natives of Africa will have far-reaching effects, not only for Africa, but for the future of the world. This is the issue of the contact of colours and civilizations, which seems destined to become a dominant issue of the twentieth century. In Asia a similar question of the contact of colours and cultures is rapidly coming to the front, and history tells us what these impacts of Asia and Europe on each other have meant in the past. These impacts it was which, renewed at various epochs, set the peoples of Europe going, and launched them on that career which has led to their domination of the world. The influence of Europe to-day on

Asia seems to be having a somewhat similar rousing effect on a colossal scale. Under the stimulus of Western ideas, Asia is being stirred and shaken from one end to the other. The rise of Japan, the awakening of India, China, the Near East, and the Malayan islands of the Pacific seem to herald another of the great movements or upheavals of history. It will depend very much on the wisdom and far-sighted policies of the European peoples, and on the growth and the success of the League of Nations in its pacific world-policy, whether this awakening of the East will be for the good or the ill of the human race as a whole.

We are concerned to-day with these racial reactions in so far as they affect Europe and Africa—a smaller question, but still a very large human question, fraught with immense possibilities for the future of our own civilization as well as that of Africa. What is wanted in Africa to-day is a wise far-sighted native policy. If we could evolve and pursue a policy which will promote the cause of civilization in Africa without injustice to the African, without injury to what is typical and specific in the African, we shall render a great service to the cause of humanity. For there is much that is good in the African and which ought to be preserved and developed. The negro and the negroid Bantu form a distinct human type which the world would be poorer without. Here in this vast continent, with its wide geographical variety and its great climatic differences, this unique human type has been fixing itself for thousands of years. It is even possible, so some anthropologists hold, that this was the original mother-type of the human race and that Africa holds the cradle of mankind. But whether this is so or not, at any rate here we have the vast result of time, which we should conserve and develop with the same high respect which we feel towards all great natural facts. This type has some wonderful characteristics. It has largely remained a child type, with a child psychology and outlook. A child-like human cannot be a bad human, for are we not in spiritual matters bidden to be like unto little children? Perhaps as a direct result of this temperament the African is the only happy human I have come across. No other race is so easily satisfied, so good-tempered, so care-free. If this had not been the case, it could scarcely have survived the intolerable evils which have weighed on it like a nightmare through the ages. A race, which could survive the immemorial practice of the witch doctor and the slave trader, and preserve its inherent simplicity and sweetness of disposition, must have some very fine moral qualities. The African easily forgets past troubles, and does not anticipate future troubles. This happy-go-lucky disposition is a great asset, but it has also its drawbacks. There is no inward incentive to improvement, there is no persistent effort in construction, and there is complete absorption in the present, its joys and sorrows. Wine, women, and song in their African forms remain the great consolations of life. No indigenous religion has been evolved, no literature, no art since the magnificent promise of the cave-men and the South African petroglyphist, no architecture since Zimbabwe (if that is African). Enough for the Africans the simple joys of village life, the dance, the tom-tom, the continual excitement of forms of fighting which cause little bloodshed. They can stand any amount of physical hardship and suffering, but when deprived of these simple enjoyments, they droop, sicken, and die. Travellers tell how for weeks the slaves would move impassively in captive gangs; but when they passed a village and heard the pleasant noises of children, the song and the dance, they would suddenly collapse and die, as if of a broken heart. These children of nature have not the inner toughness and persistence of the European, nor those social and moral incentives to progress which have built up European civilization in a comparatively short period. But they have a temperament which suits mother Africa, and which brings out the simple joys of life and deadens its pain, such as no other race possesses.

It is clear that a race so unique, and so different in its mentality and its cultures from those of Europe, requires a policy very unlike that which would suit Europeans. Nothing could be worse for Africa than the application of a policy, the object or tendency of which would be to destroy the basis of this African type, to de-Africanize the African and turn him either into a beast of the field or into a pseudo-European. And yet in the past we have tried both alternatives in our dealings with the Africans. First

we looked upon the African as essentially inferior or
sub-human, as having no soul, and as being only fit to
be a slave. As a slave he became an article of commerce, and the greatest article of export from this
continent for centuries. But the horrors of this trade
became such that the modern conscience finally re-
volted and stamped out African slavery—peacefully
in the British Empire, but in America with the convulsions of civil war and a million dead. Then we
changed to the opposite extreme. The African now
became a man and a brother. Religion and politics
combined to shape this new African policy. The
principles of the French Revolution which had
emancipated Europe were applied to Africa; liberty,
equality, and fraternity could turn bad Africans into
good Europeans. The political system of the natives
was ruthlessly destroyed in order to incorporate
them as equals into the white system. The African
was good as a potential European; his social and
political culture was bad, barbarous, and only deserv-
ing to be stamped out root and branch. In some of
the British possessions in Africa the native just emerging from barbarism was accepted as an equal citizen
with full political rights along with the whites. But
his native institutions were ruthlessly proscribed and
destroyed. The principle of equal rights was applied
in its crudest form, and while it gave the native a
semblance of equality with whites, which was little
good to him, it destroyed the basis of his African
system which was his highest good. These are the
two extreme native policies which have prevailed in

the past, and the second has been only less harmful
than the first. If Africa has to be redeemed, if Africa
has to make her own contribution to the world, if
Africa is to take her rightful place among the continents, we shall have to proceed on different lines and
evolve a policy which will not force her institutions
into an alien European mould, but which will preserve
her unity with her own past, conserve what is precious
in her past, and build her future progress and civilization on specifically African foundations. That should
be the new policy, and such a policy would be in line
with the traditions of the British Empire. As I said
on an occasion which has become historic: the British
Empire does not stand for assimilation of its peoples
into a common type, it does not stand for standardiza-
tion, but for the fullest freest development of its
peoples along their own specific lines. This principle
applies not only to its European, but also to its Asiatic
and its African constituents.

It is a significant fact that this new orientation of
African policy had its origin in South Africa, and
that its author was Cecil Rhodes in his celebrated
Glen Grey Act. Rhodes's African policy embodied
two main ideas: white settlement to supply the
steel framework and the stimulus for an enduring
civilization, and indigenous native institutions to express the specifically African character of the natives
in their future development and civilization. African
policies should arise in Africa, from the experience
of the men and women who are in daily contact with
its living problems. And it is therefore significant that

the lines on which the new Africa is being shaped are
mainly of African origin. When I call Rhodes the
original author of the new policy I do not mean that
it was his sole, individual inspiration. During the
most fruitful and successful period of his public life
he was associated with Jan Hofmeyr, who was one of
the wisest, most experienced, and far-sighted men
whom South Africa has ever produced. In evolving
his native policy Rhodes collaborated closely and continuously with Hofmeyr; and the policy in the form
it took in the celebrated Glen Grey Act was therefore
the joint product of Rhodes and Hofmeyr, of English-
and Dutch-speaking South Africans. The new orientation therefore rests on a very broad basis of African
experience.

Prior to the Glen Grey legislation it had been the
practice in South Africa, as it had been the practice
in all European-occupied territory in Africa, to rule
the natives direct through government officials,
—direct rule, as it has been called. Even where
natives were left undisturbed in the possession of
their tribal lands, the native organs of self-government were broken down and government rule was
constituted in their place. The native chiefs were
either deposed and deprived of authority, or where
use was made of them they were incorporated into the
official system and appointed as officers of the Government, from whom they derived all their authority and
in whose name that authority was exercised. The
principal innovation of Rhodes in his new legislation
was, so far as possible, to introduce indirect white

rule, and to make the natives manage their local tribal affairs. A system of native councils was inaugurated for the smaller areas, from which again delegates met to form a larger general council under the chairmanship of the resident magistrate of the area. Powers of taxation, of administration, and of recommending legislation to the Government were conferred on these councils. His second innovation was to make it possible for natives in their tribal areas to become possessed of their own separate plots of agricultural land, instead of the traditional communal holding and working of land which is the universal native system throughout Africa. Under the native system the tribe, not the individual, owns the lands, and from time to time the chief and his advisers assign to each head of a family the plot which he may cultivate for himself. This plot can be and is usually changed, so that there is no fixity of tenure, and in consequence no incentive to improve the land and to do the best with it or get the most out of it. For this communal social system of land tenure Rhodes substituted individual tenure, under certain reservations and with certain safeguards designed in the interests of the native holders themselves. A third feature of his system was a labour tax of ten shillings per annum, imposed on all native heads of families who did not go out to work beyond their district for three months in the year. The object of this tax was obvious. The whites wanted labourers, and the natives were supposed to require some inducement to go and work instead of sitting on their holdings and seeing their women work. Both in the interests of the whites and the natives, therefore, this special tax was imposed as an economic experiment. The tax, however, was unpopular with the natives from the start, and soon appeared to be an unnecessary irritation. The native men went to work quite readily or sent their young men to work for the whites. Before many years this special tax was repealed, and in later years a similar tax in the Transvaal met with the same fate. The native, although a slow worker, is not lazy, and does not require any special inducement to play his part in the economic development of the country. His main incentive is the rising scale of his needs in food and clothing, both for himself and for his often large family of children. In addition he is handicapped in South Africa by want of sufficient land for his requirements, and by the non-economic character of native farming on the whole. With his rise in the scale of civilization his needs rapidly develop, and he soon finds it necessary to supplement the scanty proceeds of his farming with the ready cash which he can earn in white employment. His economic lot, therefore, inevitably becomes more difficult, and forms a sufficient incentive to go out and work without any special means taken to force him to do so. The universal experience in Africa is that, although it takes some time at the beginning for the native to enter white employment, his rapidly growing economic needs in a white environment, and with a rising scale of living, soon make him take his full share of the burden without any

necessity to resort to special measures. The young
European communities who in other parts of the
African continent are struggling with this labour
question as their principal trouble, and who may feel
tempted to resort to the unsuccessful experiments
which we have tried and discarded in South Africa,
may take heart from our experience in South Africa
of the native as a continuously improving worker.
Dismissing therefore the question of a labour tax, we
come to consider the other features of Rhodes's Act,
their general bearing on African native policy.

His provision of individual agricultural holdings
has been a great success, and has been a principal
means of native advance where it has been adopted in
the Union. The native system of land socialism is
not only primitive but most wasteful in its working.
Why should the native farmer improve and render
productive what belongs to the community, and may
be taken away from him by the community? The
result is that these communal farm lands rapidly
deteriorate and become exhausted, and have to be
abandoned after a few years' use. Then the farm
lands shift to another area of the tribal domain where
the same process of uneconomic exhaustion is re-
peated. And in the course of years this shifting cultivation works havoc with the natural resources of the
domain; the soil is progressively exhausted; the
forests and trees disappear; the natural vegetable
covering is destroyed; soil erosion sets in; the rainfall
is lessened, and what water does fall flows off in
torrents; arid conditions arise; and the tribal lands

become a barren waste. This sad phenomenon can
be seen in one degree or another all over the
African continent. Not only in South Africa, but in
many other parts of the continent a native area or
reserve can be recognized at a distance by the obvious
general deterioration of the natural vegetation and the
soil. But for the enormous natural resources and
recuperative power of the continent, most of Africa
would by now be a howling wilderness, because of
the wasteful rural economy of its population. Unless
the carrying capacity of the land is to be gravely im-
paired in the future, steps will have to be taken everywhere to preserve the forests and the soil, and to teach
the native better methods of agriculture. Practical
agricultural education must indeed become one of
the principal subjects of native education. But
nothing will have a more far-reaching effect than a
general system of individual agricultural holdings
under proper safeguards. The economic incentive
to use properly, and to improve, what is one's own,
is more powerful than any other factor of progress.
In a world tending more and more towards general
socialism, the vague phrase of 'native socialism' may
sound attractive, but its practical effects in Africa
are everywhere devastating, and it has significantly
maintained on that continent the most backward
conditions to be found anywhere.

The main object of the Glen Grey legislation was,
however, to give the native his own institutions for
his self-development and self-government. It marks
definitely the abandonment of the older policy of

direct rule, according to which the white man's system and culture had to be imposed on the native, and native institutions had to be scrapped as barbarous. The new policy is to foster an indigenous native culture or system of cultures, and to cease to force the African into alien European moulds. As a practical policy of native government it has worked most successfully. Gradually the system of native councils and native self-government through their own tribal chiefs and elected councils has been extended from one native area to another in the Cape Province, until to-day about two-thirds of the Cape natives, or roughly over a million, fall under this system and manage their own local affairs according to their own ideas under the supervision of the European magistrates. They impose a small capitation tax of ten shillings per annum for their own local requirements, they look after their own roads, and the dipping of their cattle against disease; they teach improved agricultural methods through their own native officers; they amend their customary native law, advise the Government in regard to proposed laws in their areas, and in many other ways they look after their own local interests, find useful expression for their political energies, and get an invaluable training in disinterested public service. A sense of pride in their institutions and their own administration is rapidly developing, and, along with valuable experience in administration and public affairs, they are also acquiring a due sense of responsibility; where mistakes are made they feel satis-

fied that they have only themselves to blame. After
the new system had worked successfully and with
ever increasing efficiency for twenty-five years, I
thought the time ripe in 1920 to extend it to the whole
of the Union, and in that year an Act was passed
which gave increased powers to the councils and
authorized the Government to introduce them over
the whole Union, wherever the advance of the natives
might justify the step. A Native Affairs Commission
was at the same time appointed to advise the natives
and the Government in regard to the establishment
of new Councils, as well as in reference to all legislation affecting the natives. And it is confidently
expected that before many years have passed the
greater portion of the native population of South
Africa will be in charge of their own local affairs,
under general white supervision; and in this way
they will get an outlet for their political and administrative energies and ambitions which will give
them the necessary training for eventual participation in a wider sphere of public life.

The new departure is most far-reaching and has
come none too soon. Already the African system is
disintegrating everywhere over the whole African
continent. Many factors have combined to produce
this situation. Missionaries share the blame with
governments, the fight against the native social ideas
has been no less destructive than the deposition
of native chiefs and the institution of European
organs of government. Unfortunately the earlier
efforts of missionary enterprise were made without

any reference to, or knowledge of, the peculiar native psychology, or the light which anthropology has thrown on the past of human cultures. For the natives, religion, law, natural science, social customs and institutions, all form one blended whole, which enshrines their view of the world and of the forces governing it. Attack this complex system at any single point, and the whole is endangered. The introduction of the Christian religion meant not only the breakdown of the primitive belief in spirits, in magic and witchcraft, and the abandonment of the practice of polygamy; it meant the breakdown of the entire integral native *Weltanschauung* or outlook on life and the world. A knowledge of anthropology would have been most useful, and would have helped to conserve the native social system, while ridding it of what was barbarous or degrading. The tendency of the Christian mission has therefore on the whole been to hasten the disintegration of the native system, both in its good and its bad aspects. To this has been added the introduction of the white man's administration through his own official organs, the breakdown of the authority of the chiefs and the tribal system, and the loosening of the bonds which bind native society together, with the consequent weakening or disappearance of tribal discipline over the young men and women of the tribe. The general disintegration has been powerfully reinforced by the vast improvement in the means of transport, the opening of communications, and by labour recruitment, which have led to the movement of natives and their mix-up on a scale which would have been impossible before. The events of the Great War on the African continent have also contributed to this general disintegration. If the bonds of native tribal cohesion and authority are dissolved, the African governments will everywhere sit with vast hordes of detribalized natives on their hands, for whom the traditional restraints and the discipline of the chiefs and the elders will have no force or effect. The old social and religious sanctions will have disappeared, while no new sanctions except those of the white man's laws will have been substituted. Such a situation would be unprecedented in the history of the world and the results may well be general chaos. From time immemorial the natives of Africa have been subject to a stern, even a ruthless, discipline, and their social system has rested on the despotic authority of their chiefs. If this system breaks down and tribal discipline disappears, native society will be resolved into its human atoms, with possibilities of universal Bolshevism and chaos which no friend of the natives, or the orderly civilization of this continent, could contemplate with equanimity. Freed from all traditional moral and social discipline, the native, just emerging from barbarism, may throw all restraint to the winds. Such a breakdown should be prevented at all costs, and everything should be done to maintain in the future the authority which has guided native life in the past. In the interests of the native as well as those of the European administrations responsible for their welfare, we are called upon to retrace our steps, to take all proper measures which are still possible to restore or preserve the authority of the chiefs, and to maintain the bonds of solidarity and discipline which have supported the tribal organization of the natives in the past. This authority or discipline need not be exercised in a barbarous way, and should be shorn of all old-time cruelty and other undesirable features. But in essence it should be maintained, and under the general supervision and check of the European magistrate it should continue to be exercised. Special means should be taken to instruct chiefs in their duties, and the sons of chiefs and headmen should be trained to the proper exercise of the leadership which they may be called upon to fill. Such schools already exist, not only in South Africa, but under the Tanganyika and Uganda administrations, and may prove most helpful in preserving the traditional native chieftainship and headmanship as a vital link in the organization of native society.

The new policy is in effect enshrined in the Covenant of the League of Nations and in the mandates passed thereunder. Act 22 of the Covenant lays down that in those colonies and territories taken from the defeated Powers, which are inhabited by peoples not yet able to stand by themselves under the strenuous conditions of the modern world, there shall be applied the principle, that the well-being and development of such peoples form a sacred trust of civilization, and that this trust shall be carried out by advanced nations acting as mandatories on behalf of the League of Nations. The development of peoples, not yet able to stand by themselves, can only mean the progress and civilization of these backward peoples in accordance with their own institutions, customs, and ideas, in so far as these are not incompatible with the ideals of civilization. That this was the plain meaning and intention of the article I can state with some authority, as I was in a measure responsible for this mandate principle and for its formulation in article 22 of the Covenant. This article enshrines a policy and a principle which is not only in consonance with common sense, but which has already been tested in practice on a fairly large scale, and which in future ought to govern universally the contacts between European and other less advanced peoples.

It may be of some interest to indicate briefly how this policy is being applied in a mandated territory like Tanganyika. The foundation of the system is the maintenance and building up of the authority of the chiefs in their various ranks. Their sons receive special training in a school for the sons of chiefs, intended to fit them for their future duties. Their office is hereditary, but deposition and popular election are both possible in accordance with native ideas. The chief is responsible for the administration of his tribe, maintains order and good government within its area, and prevents the commission of offences. The heads of families pay an annual tax of ten shillings, which goes into the tribal treasury, from which a fixed amount is paid to the chief for his maintenance, the balance being devoted to tribal purposes. The chief can issue orders for a large number of purposes, such as prohibiting or controlling the manufacture and consumption of intoxicating liquors, preventing the pollution of the water in any stream, controlling migration of natives to or from his area, and requiring any native to cultivate land in such a way and with such crops as will secure a proper supply of food for him and his family. He may also make rules imposing fines and other penalties for the enforcement of his orders. Native courts are also instituted, administering native law and custom in both civil and criminal cases between natives within a certain jurisdiction; and from their decisions or sentences appeals lie ultimately to a white authority, who has also to confirm certain criminal sentences before their execution.

The white administration remains responsible for the larger functions of government, such as the combating of human and animal diseases, the organization of education, the improvement of agriculture, and the construction of public works, and maintains a staff for these and similar purposes. But all the purely tribal concerns are left to the chief and his counsellors whose actions are supervised by the white officer only in certain cases intended to prevent abuses. The native system may not be as efficient and incorruptible as direct white rule would be, but a certain amount of inefficiency or even injustice, according to white ideas, is excusable, so long as the natives are trained to govern themselves according to their own ideas, and bear the responsibility for their own small mistakes. In this way they learn to stand by themselves, and will in the long run be trained to do all their own local government work. It is not only the training in self-government that will benefit them. They will develop the sense of responsibility which goes with it, and which is in itself one of the most valuable lessons of life. In looking after their own concerns they will, in addition, cultivate a sense of pride in their own system and increase their self-respect. And, above all, they will develop an active interest in their own public affairs, which will be of enormous moral and social value. The white man does the native a grave injury by doing everything for him in the way of government, and thereby depriving his life of all public interest. Gone is the excitement of his petty wars ; and if in addition there is the repression of all his former public activities and the suppression of his native values, we must expect a sense of frustration which will take all the zest out of his life. The question has even been raised whether the white man's rule, in taking all the interest out of native life, is not responsible for that decadence, lowered birth-rate, and slow petering out which we see in the case of many primitive peoples. At any rate the new policy of native self-government will provide the natives with plenty of bones to chew at and plenty of matter to wrangle over—and they do love to talk and dispute *ad infinitum*—and in that way help to fill their otherwise empty lives with interest.

Another important consequence will follow from this system of native institutions. Wherever Euro-

peans and natives live in the same country, it will
mean separate parallel institutions for the two. The
old practice mixed up black with white in the same
institutions; and nothing else was possible, after the
native institutions and traditions had been carelessly
or deliberately destroyed. But in the new plan there
will be what is called in South Africa 'segregation'—
separate institutions for the two elements of the
population, living in their own separate areas. Separate institutions involve territorial segregation of the
white and black. If they live mixed up together it is
not practicable to sort them out under separate
institutions of their own. Institutional segregation
carries with it territorial segregation. The new policy
therefore gives the native his own traditional institutions on land which is set aside for his exclusive
occupation. For agricultural and pastoral natives,
living their tribal life, large areas or reserves are set
aside, adequate for their present and future needs.
In not setting aside sufficient such areas in South
Africa in the past we committed a grievous mistake,
which is at the root of most of our difficulties in
native policy. For urbanized natives, on the other
hand, who live, not under tribal conditions but as
domestic servants or industrial workers in white
areas, there are set aside native villages or locations,
adjoining to the European towns. In both rural
reserves and town locations the natives take a
part in or run their own local self-government.
Such is the practice now in vogue in South Africa
and it is likely to develop still further, and to

spread all over Africa where white and black live and work together in the same countries. For residential and local government purposes a clean cleavage is becoming ever more marked, the white portion of the population living under more advanced European institutions, while the natives next door maintain their simpler indigenous system. This separation is imperative, not only in the interests of a native culture, and to prevent native traditions and institutions from being swamped by the more powerful organization of the whites, but also for other important purposes, such as public health, racial purity, and public good order. The mixing up of two such alien elements as white and black leads to unhappy social results—racial miscegenation, moral deterioration of both, racial antipathy and clashes, and to many other forms of social evil. In these great matters of race, colour, and culture, residential separation and parallel institutions alone can do justice to the ideals of both sections of the population. The system is accepted and welcomed by the vast majority of natives; but it is resented by a small educated minority who claim 'equal rights' with the whites. It is, however, evident that the proper place of the educated minority of the natives is with the rest of their people, of whom they are the natural leaders, and from whom they should not in any way be dissociated.

Far more difficult questions arise on the industrial plane. It is not practicable to separate black and white in industry, and their working together in the same industry and in the same works leads to a certain amount of competition and friction and antagonism, for which no solution has yet been found. Unhappy attempts have been made in South Africa to introduce a colour bar, and an Act of that nature is actually on the Statute book, but happily no attempt has yet been made to apply it in practice. It empowers the Government to set aside separate spheres of work for the native and the non-native, the object being to confine the native to the more or less unskilled occupations or grades of work. The inherent economic difficulties of such a distribution of industrial functions, the universal objection of the native workers, and the sense of fair-play among the whites will make its practical application virtually impossible. No statutory barrier of that kind should be placed on the native who wishes to raise himself in the scale of civilization, nor could it be maintained for long against the weight of modern public opinion. As a worker the white man should be able to hold his own in competition with the native. Industrial as distinguished from territorial segregation would be both impracticable and an offence against the modern conscience.

There remains the big question how far the parallelism of native and white institutions is to go? Is it to be confined to local government, or is it to go all the way, up to the level of full political or parliamentary government? Should black and white co-operate in the same parliamentary institutions of the country? If so, should they have separate representa-

tives in the same parliamentary institutions? Few
acquainted with the facts and the difficulties can
profess to see clear daylight in the tangle of this
problem. In the older practice, embodied in the
constitution of the former Cape Colony and in many
other colonial institutions, political equality between
the different races on the basis of a complete mixture
of political rights was recognized. Justice is colour-
blind and recognizes no political differences on
grounds of colour or race. Hence the formula of
equal 'rights for all civilized men' with which the
name of Rhodes is identified, and which represents
the traditional British policy. That policy, however,
arose at a time when the doctrine of native parallelism had not yet emerged, when native institutions
were proscribed as barbarous, and the only place for
the civilized native was therefore in the white man's
system and the white man's institutions. The
question is whether the new principle makes, or
should make, any difference to the old tradition of
mixed and equal political rights in the same parliamentary institutions. I notice that the Hilton Young
Commission, after having made a powerful plea for
separate native institutions for local government
purposes, pause when they come up against the
question of parliamentary institutions, and in the
end leave the question over for the future.

'If' (they say), 'the idea of parallel development is accepted,
then it follows that it is desirable to keep the way open as long
as possible for the maximum measure of political segregation.
This suggests that political development for the native and

the settled areas should be carried forward on separate lines—native and British respectively—as far as possible.'[1]

Lord Lugard, in dealing with the question of equal rights in relation to colour, lays down the following proposition which a former President of the United States of America approved of:

'Here, then,' (he says), 'is the true conception of the inter-relation of colour: complete uniformity in ideals, absolute equality in the paths of knowledge and culture, equal opportunity for those who strive, equal administration for those who achieve; in matters social and racial a separate path, each pursuing his own inherited traditions, preserving his own race-purity and race-pride; equality in things spiritual, agreed difference in the physical and material.'[2]

An admirable statement of the principle to which I think all fair-minded men will agree. But you notice once more the silence about political rights.

I do not think there can be, or that at bottom there is, among those who have given the subject serious attention, any doubt that in the supreme legislature of a country with a mixed population all classes and colours should have representation. It is repugnant to our civilized European ideas that the weaker in a community should not be heard or should go without representation, either by themselves or through European spokesmen, where their interests are concerned. There can be but one sovereign body in a country, and that body should represent the weaker no less than the stronger. To that extent there should be agreement. As to the mode of representa-

---

[1] Cmd. 3234, p. 84.   [2] *Dual Mandate*, p. 87

tion of colour in the supreme parliament there can be legitimate difference of opinion. The older practice was to give equal rights in the sense of mixed representation, the same member of the legislature representing mixed bodies of white and native voters alike. The new policy of segregation of political rights would seem to point to separate representation for the colours in the same parliament so that white and native voters would vote in separate constituencies for separate representatives. There would still be equal political rights, and the Rhodes ideal in that sense would not be affected, but they would be exercised separately or communally. In South Africa, which, owing to the advanced condition of its natives, has become a sort of cockpit for race issues, we started with the older system of mixed constituencies in the Cape Colony, and this system is embodied and entrenched in the Act of Union which forms our Constitution. The present Government have proposed to scrap this system for the future, and to give separate representation in Parliament to native and non-native voters. A policy which might have been easy and, from certain points of view, even commendable, with a clean slate before us, has become enormously difficult because of what has been done in the past, and the justifiable fervour with which the Cape natives cling to their vested rights, which they have enjoyed for three-quarters of a century. A battle royal is still proceeding on this and cognate issues affecting the political rights of the natives, and it will require all the wisdom and patience which we can command in South Africa if we are to reach a generally acceptable solution. If we had to do only with the tribal native voters the question would not be so difficult, and the application of the general segregation principle to the particular case of political rights might be justified. Unfortunately very large numbers of detribalized natives are spread all over the Cape, and are no longer resident or registered in the native areas. These urbanized natives living among the whites constitute the real crux, and it is a difficulty which goes far beyond the political issue. They raise a problem for the whole principle of segregation, as they claim to be civilized and Europeanized, and do not wish to be thrust back into the seclusion of their former tribal associations, or to forgo their new place in the sun among the whites. With the application of strict education and civilization tests it would probably be the better course to allow them to exercise their political rights along with the whites. Were it not for this case of the urbanized or detribalized natives, the colour problem, not only in South Africa but elsewhere in Africa, would be shorn of most of its difficulties. And the situation in South Africa is therefore a lesson to all the younger British communities farther north to prevent as much as possible the detachment of the native from his tribal connexion, and to enforce from the very start the system of segregation with its conservation of separate native institutions.

In conclusion I wish to refer to an apparent discrepancy between this lecture and my previous one.

In that lecture I stressed the importance of white settlement in Africa as a potent means of furthering native progress and civilization. I pointed out that enduring contact with the white man's civilization is the surest way to civilize the native. In this lecture I have emphasized the importance of preserving native institutions, of keeping intact as far as possible the native system of organization and social discipline. It may be thought that there is a clash between these two aims, and that civilization by white contact must inevitably lead to the undermining and ultimately to the destruction of the native culture and social system. This, however, is not so. So long as there is territorial segregation, so long as the native family home is not with the white man but in his own area, so long the native organization will not be materially affected. While the native may come voluntarily out of his own area for a limited period every year to work with a white employer, he will leave his wife and children behind in their native home. The family life in the native home will continue on the traditional lines; the routine of the family and of the tribe will not be altered in any material respect. The male adults, father and sons, will no doubt imbibe new ideas in their white employment, but their social system will not suffer on that account. It is only when segregation breaks down, when the whole family migrates from the tribal home and out of the tribal jurisdiction to the white man's farm or the white man's town, that the tribal bond is snapped, and the traditional system falls into decay. And it is this migration of the native family, of the females and children, to the farms and the towns which should be prevented. As soon as this migration is permitted the process commences which ends in the urbanized detribalized native and the disappearance of the native organization. It is not white employment of the native males that works the mischief, but the abandonment of the native tribal home by the women and children. This the law should vigorously prevent, and the system—whether it is administered through passes or in any other way—should only allow the residence of males for limited periods, and for purposes of employment among the whites. If this is done there will be no serious danger that the indigenous native system will be unduly affected.

At the same time I wish to point out that the prevention of this migration will be no easy task, even where ample tribal lands are guaranteed to the natives. The whites like to have the families of their native servants with them. It means more continuous and less broken periods of labour, and it means more satisfied labourers. It means, moreover, the use of the women and children for such work as they are fit for. These are considerable advantages, and the white employers will not be very keen to carry out a law against them. On the other hand, the native also very often likes to get away from the jurisdiction of the chief and the discipline of the tribe, and prefers to have his women and his children around him in his daily life. For the native the pressure to break away from the old bonds and live with his white master is thus very

great. We have seen the process at work in South
Africa. When the white emigrants entered and occupied Natal, they found the entire territory between
Zululand and Pondoland unoccupied; it had been
laid bare and made a waste buffer between these two
powerful native states. But no sooner had the whites
settled in this empty area, than native deserters, dissatisfied with the harsh rule of their chiefs, began to
arrive and to settle as servants among the whites.
And to-day, through this wholly voluntary migration,
the province of Natal has a very large native population. It was not a case of the natives not having
sufficient fertile lands for their own use. Zululand is
one of the most fertile parts of South Africa, and it
was and remains comparatively thinly populated.
White employment, white protection, the freedom of
the white man's rule compared to the discipline of the
native chief and the jurisdiction of the tribe have been
the potent factors in bringing about this migration.
And they will continue to operate in all parts of Africa
where whites settle down. In the old Cape Colony
one frontier after another was drawn by the Cape
governors between the white settlements and the
native tribes, and migration from the one to the other
was prohibited under stern penalties. But the system
was for ever breaking down. The whites like to have
native servants; the natives prefer to have white
masters, and this double economic attraction has
proved too much for any prohibitory law.

There is, however, no reason why segregation, although it has broken down in South Africa in the

past, should not be a workable and enforceable system in the future. The power of Government and the reach of the law are to-day very different from what they were under the primitive nomadic conditions of the old Cape frontier. The system of native administration is to-day so ramified and pervasive, the policeman is so ubiquitous, that segregation can be tried under far more favourable conditions than existed in South Africa in the past. The young countries to the north can start with a clean slate. They can learn from the mistakes which we made in South Africa, and can *ab initio* reserve ample lands for the natives to live and work on. They can check the abuses of the chiefs, and can effectively supervise the working of the native system, both in its administrative and judicial aspects. Witchcraft can be fought, official injustice and corruption can be largely prevented, schools can be established, and the simplest amenities of civilized life can be introduced, in the native villages and tribal areas. The position is really very different from what it was generations ago, and the inducements for native families to remain on their tribal lands are such, or can be made such, that a segregation law will become comparatively easy to carry out. The women and children will continue to carry on their native life at home, will continue to work in the homes and in the fields as they have done from the immemorial past. The men, instead of lying in the sun, or brawling over their beer, or indulging in the dangerous sport of tribal warfare, will go out to work, and supplement the family income and render tolerable a weight which under the new conditions is becoming more and more difficult for the women and children. They should never be away long, and the physical and moral life of the family and the tribe need not suffer because of the short periods of absence. Theorists may pick holes in such a system, but there is no practical reason why it should not work in practice. There is no break in the communal village life, but among the men the thin end of the industrial wedge is quietly introduced, and they rightly become the bread-winners which they have seldom or never been. Such a system has great redeeming features, and compares more than favourably with the old ways, which meant absolute stagnation for the men, and virtual slavery for the women. It represents a compromise between the native routine of the past and the white man's industrial system, which may work tolerably well in the future. Without breaking down what is good in the native system, it will graft on to it a wholesome economic development, which will yet not disturb too deeply the traditional ways of mother Africa. The white man's civilization and the steadily progressing native culture will live side by side and react on each other, and the problems of their contact will provide a fruitful theme for the statesmen of the future.

IV
WORLD-PEACE

WORLD-PEACE

THE object which Rhodes had in view in making his famous will is best brought out in the original draft which he made when he was a young man of twenty-four, and had his life still before him and his great fortune to make. In this curious document he expresses his object as being 'the foundation of so great a Power as hereafter to render wars impossible and to promote the best interests of humanity'. The Power he meant was stated to be a greatly expanded British Empire, with the U.S.A. once more reunited to it. In the final draft of his will, made twenty-two years afterwards, he emphasizes the following among his other objects, viz. 'the advantage to the colonies as well as to England of the retention of the unity of the Empire'. In spite of this emphasis on the unity of the Empire, this final draft retained the American scholarships, and included also the German scholar-ships. It is therefore a fair inference that Rhodes's final vision was not confined to the British Empire, but that he continued to cherish the ideal of world peace and the best interests of humanity at large. It was for the purpose of achieving this larger ideal that he wished to bring together the scholars of what he considered the three leading world-peoples. Through the association of the future potential leaders of these peoples at the same great school, he wished to pro-mote international understanding, and thereby to lay the foundations for world-peace. World-peace and human betterment remained his real ideals, and the scholarship scheme was to be the means to their realization.

While Rhodes was planning for world-peace in his will, the terrible seeds of the future were germinating in that placid Victorian world, and within a short span of years after his death the greatest war in history had broken out. To deepen the irony, the very peoples whom he had singled out and had associated in his will as the joint guarantors of future peace were the principal protagonists against each other. Not only was his dream falsified here, but, when the war was over, an organization for world-peace was created very different from that which Rhodes had originally envisaged. In spite of this, however, his main object and his plan for its attainment remain unaffected, and the tremendous developments referred to have not rendered his will by any means obsolete. The scholarship scheme will still remain a potent and permanent means to further the great ideal of world-peace through human understanding. Hence, in discussing the main policies of Rhodes, it is by no means out of place to discuss what is to-day the dominant issue of world politics. I therefore make no apology for taking the subject of world-peace as my theme to-day.

The new institution for world-peace—the League of Nations—came into the world under the gravest handicaps. It was almost killed by the initial ridicule with which its appearance was hailed. It looked so small and puny, so utterly unequal to the terrible situations which might confront it, that few were prepared to take it seriously. It was said to be the scheme of the idealists, and, even as such, but a travesty of the great hopes and expectations born of the world-war. Hard-headed practical men were inclined to be sceptical; the old diplomatic order sneered; the powers-that-be smiled at this hope of the world. Some thought the scheme too far-reaching and ambitious; others again thought it was too cumbrous and impracticable, and that its machinery would never function in a real crisis. Many were openly hostile, called it a sham and a delusion, mere dope for the unsuspecting, to lull them into a false sense of security. In spite of the League the cry for security went up all over Europe, from people who evidently thought that there was no security to be looked for from the League. I point to this original attitude towards the League in order to emphasize the great change that has taken place in public opinion within the last ten years. There are still sceptics, but they are not so loud; they are on the defensive. The Council and the Assembly of the League have not become the refuge for pompous nonentities as was expected; the Prime Ministers and Foreign Ministers of Europe find it to their advantage to be present at the sessions and to make use of the League as the greatest platform in the world from which to address the public. In spite of a chequered record and many incidental failures, it has steadily made good and established itself, until to-day it is universally accepted as an indispensable organ of international relations. The founders have builded better than they knew; the experiment has worked better than was expected; and the growing influence of the League and the more respectful attitude adopted towards it are a tribute to its steadily growing success. We have passed out of the era of idle compliments and covert sneers; the political realists have begun to realize that there is something in the thing, and that it is not one more idealistic bubble which is destined to be pricked in the march of events. Friends of the League, again, have no reason to be dissatisfied with the progress made, and feel justified in looking to the future with renewed hope, and in going forward with a firmer determination than ever to make of the League a powerful factor in human progress.

The change in public opinion to which I have referred is a matter of the greatest significance. The original lukewarmness and scepticism with which the League was received were intelligible and in a sense excusable. It was a new fact, the real significance of which was not likely to be easily realized by conservative-minded people. What was more, it purported to be the beginning of a new order of things in a world where innovations were up against a very tough old order. Remembering the prevailing ideas of the Victorian era, and the views of international law and relations to which people were accustomed, it is nothing short of amazing, that in the short span of years which has elapsed since the Great War, public opinion has come to

accept so revolutionary a departure as that which
the League of Nations stands for. The sovereign
powers of Europe and the world have been brought
to sit round a table as a regular constitutional routine,
to discuss their most intimate affairs with each
other, to submit their legal differences to a court of
international justice, and their political or national
differences to mediation or conciliation boards. They
have made the use of that great weapon of national
aggrandizement—war—almost impossible, and they
have finally renounced its use as an instrument of
national policy. They have voluntarily agreed to
limit their sovereign rights in deference to the interests of the international family of which they
recognize themselves to be members. Difficult as this
grand renunciation must be to those who only yester-
day believed firmly that national power and influence depended on military power and on the war
weapon, they are to-day proceeding slowly to the
still harder step of reducing their armies and navies
as a pledge of their good faith and their loyalty to the
new order of things. Looked at in its true light, in the
light of the ages and of the time-honoured ideas and
practice of mankind, we are beholding an amazing
thing—we are witnessing one of the great miracles of
history. Of course the miracle has only become possible because of the unexampled sufferings through
which this generation has passed, because even the
most hardened sinner is sick at heart at the sorrows
and sufferings which have been our lot, and because
only a moral or political lunatic could dare to obstruct

a universal movement which calls a halt to such calamities. But still it is essentially a miracle that we are witnessing in the great peace movement of our day. One incident, illustrating the far-reaching character of the changes now setting in, stands out very clearly in my memory. When towards the end of 1918 I showed Lord Bryce the draft for a League of Nations which I had made, and the main principles of which were afterwards embodied in the Covenant, that wise man, in spite of his convinced idealism, asked me whether I really thought it possible that the Great Powers would accept a scheme involving such limitations on their sovereign rights. To him it seemed entirely unlikely that they would reconcile themselves to such a surrender. And yet that is exactly what they have since done. The League may be a difficult scheme to work, but the significant thing is that the Great Powers have pledged themselves to work it, that they have agreed to renounce their free choice of action and bound themselves to what amounts in effect to a consultative parliament of the world. By the side of that great decision and the enormous step in advance which it means, any small failures to live up to the great decision, any small lapses on the part of the League, are trifling indeed. The great choice is made, the great renunciation is over, and mankind has as it were at one bound, and in the short space of ten years, jumped from the old order to the new, across a gulf which may yet prove to be the greatest break or divide in human history. Let us not, in our first dissatisfaction or indignation over occasional failures of the League to live up to its great ideal, lose sight of this really all-important fact; let us not lose our real sense of values or our right perspective. The advance actually and incontestably made is so great that no incidental error or lapse on the part of the League can seriously detract from it. There is no looking back or retracing of steps possible any more —we can only move forward. He who recants and proceeds to defy the League will be a traitor and a law-breaker to a legally established order, and will be dealt with on that basis. What has been done can never be undone. One epoch closes in the history of the world and another opens.

Mind you, I do not say that there will be no more wars. But this I do say, that any future wars will rest on an entirely different basis from that on which past wars have rested, and will meet with a different human attitude from that in which past wars were regarded. Past wars, even the most immoral and indefensible, were legal; they were sanctioned by international usage and law. As great legal acts of national policy they commanded the high devotion of private citizens, they called forth the most exalted heroisms; they were consecrated by the highest enthusiasm and covered by a blaze of glory. All the loyalties and heroisms of which human nature was capable, all the glory and romance which could thrill the human soul deepest, were connected with war. It will be so no longer. Henceforth, by an inevitable process, war follows the chivalry of feudalism into the limbo of the past. If it shows its face, it will be without the mask of romance which made it so attractive in the past; it will appear to be the cruel, accursed, illegal thing that it really is; the nation that resorts to it will be branded as a public danger and nuisance by the general consensus of opinion. Public opinion will frown on it, and it will be a sordid, tawdry affair. The warlike Don Quixote of the future will meet with laughter and ridicule, and if he persists he will run the risk of condign punishment at the hands of the nations. What is more: the future is to those nations who unreservedly accept the new situation. The wise and prudent nations will quietly and deliberately shape their course according to the new international system; will gradually ease their own burdens and reduce their war establishments. The emotional and imprudent on the other hand may continue to think along the old lines, wasting their treasure and their substance to no purpose, sacrificing their national well-being, and running the risk of eventually bumping their heads severely. But in either case the ultimate result is a foregone conclusion, and in time war will inevitably disappear from the civilized practice of the world.

This expectation is in advance of present public opinion, but I have no doubt whatever that my reading of the situation is essentially correct; that war, even if it cannot yet be said to be dead, is finally doomed, and that no possible setback in the fortunes of the League can seriously affect the ultimate result. In the meantime the widespread spirit of criticism, and even of hostility, which has accompanied the progress of the League during the last ten years has on the whole proved rather helpful than otherwise to it. It has prevented an attitude of self-satisfaction from arising inside the League; it has rendered impossible a spirit of complacency which would have been fatal at the present stage. Nothing would have been worse or more dangerous than to have rested satisfied with the *status quo* and to have looked upon the League as a final achievement and as if the last word had been said. For at present the League is but a step in the right direction—although a most epoch-making step—and it will have to cover a long road to its goal of world-peace and human well-being. The critical attitude towards the League has acted as a spur to further thought and experiment, and has prevented the present inchoate stage from being stereotyped as in any sense final. The League in its methods and procedure is a grand experiment, perhaps the greatest ever traced in history; perhaps an experiment destined to become the greatest institution in human government. But at present and for decades to come, it will be in the experimental developing stage. We are still in the creative, formative stage, and dare not rest satisfied with the results already achieved. And the deep note of criticism and scepticism continues to act as an incentive to further unremitting effort and progress.

Great ideas are wonderful things. They are the real dynamics of individual and social advance.

Once a great idea has appeared in concrete form it seems to be well-nigh indestructible. It resembles a Mendelian factor which, once achieved, can never be undone again—at any rate not in the ordinary course of events. The buffeting which a great fruitful idea receives from criticism or otherwise only helps it along all the more. What is true and fruitful and constructive in it is thereby disengaged and freed from the merely temporary and adventitious, and becomes in consequence all the more effective. That is one of the reasons why great ideas have often been so potent in history, in spite of the violent opposition which they have usually encountered. In their fruitful truth they contain the energy of their own propulsion: they move by their own momentum, so to speak. And in the end they become irresistible. Their appeal, their contacts are universal, they become atmospheric, they infect minds in all directions, and they win through by their own infectiousness and irresistible power and driving force. The League of Nations belongs to this fruitful order of ideas. If it had not, it might never have survived the enormous difficulties which surrounded its origin and progress, and it would never have risen as it has done, Antaeus-like, fresh and stronger from every fall and every set-back.

Let me briefly refer to some of those serious difficulties which it has encountered. One of the earliest criticisms levelled against it was that it was the conception and the work of unpractical idealists and enthusiasts, who had little regard to the hard facts of the practical world. This criticism was only too widely believed and did, and still is doing, an enormous amount of harm. That the Covenant was largely the work of a small band of so-called idealists at the Peace Conference I freely admit—and all honour to them for their achievement. But that the scheme was visionary or out of relation to the actual world situation I stoutly deny. Woodrow Wilson and his co-workers were not only idealists but practical men who recognized that the moment for action had come, and who resolutely saw the business through in spite of all the criticism and scepticism which was the prevailing attitude towards the League idea at Paris. If they too had failed, if this unique opportunity had been missed, the Peace might have become an unmitigated disaster. There is no saying when another chance might have occurred again, and we might in this generation have continued to be weighed down by the burden of the Peace Treaty, without the vision of world-peace which, under the Covenant, has been the one ray of hope and the one redeeming feature of an otherwise hopeless situation. Now, at any rate, the golden promise of world-peace has at last been saved out of the wreck of the War and the Peace, and the time may come when the world will recognize that the authors of the Covenant were the only really practical people at the Peace Conference.

So far from the Covenant being visionary or out of relation to the facts and the exigencies of the time, it is clear beyond all doubt that the Covenant sprang out of the actual situation at the end of the war, and

the temper it had created in the minds of men. There
was an unspeakable longing that this horror might be
the last of its kind; there was the well-grounded fear
for the future that another great war might be the
end of the human race; and there was the deep feeling
that only the assured hope of future world-peace
could justify the endless sufferings through which
mankind had passed in the Great War. The Covenant
was the creative birth which issued out of those bitter
pains of the human race. If ever a great result arose
directly out of the necessities of a terrible situation,
the Covenant was *par excellence* such a birth of time.
Its form was of course shaped by the minds and
thoughts of those who elaborated it; its substance, its
real being was the direct response to the measureless
woes and the boundless hopes of the human race at
the end of the world-war. It was the child of the
human race and of no individual or set of individuals.
The movement of history is often creative in the true
sense. Great events, interacting with the human spirit
on a vast scale, become pregnant with new meaning,
and out of the clashes, the sorrows and sufferings of
the time, arise vague anticipations of a new order;
then suddenly, unexpectedly, and as if by sheer acci-
dent, there comes the embodiment of some great hope
or thought, which, once formulated, acquires an independent existence and movement of its own, and
becomes a new force in the world. It is only a shallow
reading of history which misses this deeper creative
character, which attributes all large-scale developments to personal scheming, and neglects the im-

mense movement of the imponderables, which has been the main factor.

The essence of the Covenant and the most valuable and important thing in it is just its main conception that there shall be an organized system of conference and discussion between the States for the promotion of understanding and the prevention of war. The particular machinery adopted to secure world-peace is of minor importance in comparison. The particular methods will change and will be improved with experience; those settled on in the first instance need not be looked upon as more than provisional. But the main idea, materialized and regularized in a conference system, has a potency and a value all its own, and is probably the chief asset of the League. The conference system has become firmly established within the last ten years, and is functioning regularly; and so the main idea of the League has rooted itself in the public system of Europe, and bids fair to become the most important organ of it. How important such a regular conference system in itself is for the promotion of peace must be patent to all who remember the chaos in diplomacy which arose in July 1914 as the prelude to the Great War—a chaos which, in my opinion, became the determining cause of that catastrophe. From this point of view, nothing can be more instructive than to compare the present conference system of the League with the methods in vogue before the Great War. To any one looking into the matter it must be clear that a wide gulf already divides us from the international practice of the pre-war era. Nothing can bring home to us more clearly the real advance that the League has already meant in the public life of the world than a look back on that mad world of 1914. I would advise every serious student of the League system to do what I did last year, that is, to read once more through the diplomatic correspondence and the negotiations between the Great Powers which preceded the outbreak of the Great War. Never before had the conviction been borne in upon me so strongly that it was not so much the malign intent of governments as the faultiness of the diplomatic methods which led to that tragedy. It was a failure in diplomatic machinery even more than in human ability or goodwill. The popular idea fostered during the war period for propaganda purposes, that A was the devil of the piece or B it was who deliberately planned the war, has long since been shown to be devoid of substantial truth. There was more drifting than planning at that crisis of our fate. True, there had been a long era of large-scale arming for national aggrandizement or defence, for which a dreadful responsibility rested on all concerned, but no one was big enough or mad enough deliberately to press the button at the last. And when finally a far-off shot by a madman at Sarajevo fired the train, there was no statesman big or sane enough in the wide world to stop the consequences. Human error and failure had created a situation which acted like blind fate, with which intelligence found it impossible to cope successfully in the end. There followed a week of frenzied correspondence and diplomacy. Through a thick fog of suspicion, misunderstanding, and confusion, the Powers were bombarding one another with a barrage of correspondence at long range. Sir Edward Grey, seeing the futility of it all, made desperate efforts to collect them round a table and make them reason together. But it was too late, and the confusion grew as terror, panic, and the traditional war complexes began to overpower the mass mind of Europe. You cannot improvise the machinery of reason in the last moments of chaos. And so in utter confusion and helplessness Europe stumbled, and could not but stumble, in darkness into the abyss. The situation is very different to-day, whatever the pessimists may say. My impression is strong that if the machinery of conference and direct consultation and confrontation such as now exists in the League had been functioning normally in July 1914, the outbreak of the Great War could have been avoided, but not otherwise. And I feel convinced that, in spite of its inherent weakness and its many incidental failures, the League in its present constitution and practice is a real guarantee against a recurrence of such a frenzied crisis and such a catastrophe as overtook the world fifteen years ago. Its regular and settled methods will help the world more effectively than all the alliances and balances of power and groupings of the pre-war era. And after all that is the true view and the real justification of the League. It is, and becomes more and more, an habitual organized system of international conference, it supplies the very machinery, the absence of which proved fatal in 1914; and while it may not prevent the sporadic outbreak of small wars on the outer fringe of civilization, it will certainly render a crisis such as that of 1914 impossible.

I have laboured this point because critics are more apt to fasten on to details than to grasp the essentials of the League system. Holes can be picked almost everywhere in the details of its machinery; but its main conception, its central conference system is in my opinion unassailable. And if that system continues to grow at the present rate, and to root itself sufficiently deeply in the public life of civilization, war as an instrument of national policy is certainly doomed in the long run. The League has become an established institution with its regular routine. There is all the difference in the world between such an institution and a mere declaration of policy such as the Kellogg Peace Pact. An institution is organic, it is a living, growing entity; it roots itself ever more deeply into the soil of life; it has a definiteness, a materiality, an assurance of growth and continuance and security, such as no mere idea or abstract principle can aspire to. The conference system, incarnated in an established institution which becomes ever more closely associated with the international life of the world, has a stability and acquires a prestige and authority which makes it a far more powerful force in human affairs than any abstract declaration could ever possibly be. The declaration may be good and useful, but it could never take the place of the living functioning institution. The function requires a structure.

Passing on now to another aspect of the League system, I wish to draw attention to its pacific methods as distinct from its pacific aims. The League aims at peace by essentially peaceful methods. Its main work is done through the international court, arbitration bodies, and conciliation conferences in which the parties to a dispute take part. To look upon the League as a League of force, as an organization for making war upon an international wrongdoer or disturber of the peace, is completely to misunderstand its true nature. The issue as to the real nature of the League was faced and fought out in the Commission of the Peace Conference appointed to frame the Covenant. One school held that the methods of the League should be essentially peaceful, that consultation and conference was of its very essence, and that to endow it with a war staff and an international force would not only detract from its fundamental idea, but also seriously deflect it from its true mission and in the end injure its work. This was the Anglo-American view, whose advocates held tenaciously to the position that the League was not a repetition of an old device, and was not a war-machine to guarantee peace, but an essentially new method and procedure, a system of conference, arbitration, and conciliation to prevent war. It was recognized that these pacific methods might fail in their object, but so might also the opposite method of an organization of war in order to prevent war. And it was urged that the pacific methods were far less likely to lead to complications and to the eventual damage of the League, and would prevent it from being regarded as a warlike combination of a group of Powers or sort of Holy Alliance. The thesis of the French school was that the League in effect was an organization to guarantee the peace settlement, and they argued that a league for this purpose without a general staff and an international force to back up its decisions would be ineffective. If the League was really going to be a new power and vital influence in international affairs, if its decisions had to be respected and international peace maintained, it was necessary for it to carry out its policy with its own force, if necessary. Without such a force it would not be respected or obeyed, and it might easily degenerate into a debating society, devoid of all authority or prestige. In this fundamental argument as to the future character of the League, the Anglo-American view prevailed, and all attempts to establish an international war-staff and an international force were defeated. As the Covenant was framed, the League was confined to pacific methods, the only exception to this rule being the unfortunate Art. 10, which guarantees the sovereignty and the territory of the members of the League. This Article, which proved the chief stumbling-block against the entry of the U.S.A. into the League, was subsequently attacked in the Assembly of the League, and a proposal was made to water down its effect. It can only be looked upon as an exception to the real trend and purpose of the League, and in time no doubt it will be modified. The economic boycott under Art. 16 is the only sanction with which the League was provided, and an aggressor who defies an arbitration award or a unanimous decision of this Council of the League has to face the severance of commercial and trade relations with the members of the League, and may in that way be subjected to the severest economic penalties. But the employment of force or the resort to war by the members of the League in such a case is not made compulsory by the terms of the Covenant. It was thought that the severance of financial and commercial intercourse was such a drastic punishment to a modern state that nothing more was really required in the nature of a sanction. It might be a difficult sanction to apply in practice, but the declaration of war against an aggressor under the Covenant would certainly be an even more difficult and dangerous procedure.

Although the attempt to establish the League on a military basis was thus defeated, the French school and their Continental supporters were never satisfied with the result, and continued to look upon the League as now constituted as being too weak to provide real 'security'. They therefore returned to the charge in the Assembly of 1923 and got the Protocol accepted by that Assembly. On a change of Government in Great Britain the following year, the Protocol was in turn vetoed, and the original constitution of the League therefore remained intact. I look upon this as a matter of first-class importance, and always considered the Protocol as a real calamity from the League point of view. Mr. Henderson has made amends for this early mistake by his fine performance in bringing the whole British Empire under the Optional Clause of the International Court. The Protocol was in effect an all-in arbitration system for members of the League, with a mutual guarantee of military and naval force by the members in order to carry out the arbitral awards against any aggressor under the Protocol. It was a most ambitious attempt to end war finally and to constitute the League a military organization for the purpose. A new war association was to be created in order to fight war. Satan was to be enlisted to fight sin. To me this seemed a grave departure from the sacred League ideal, which was not merely to end war, but to end it in a new way, in a way which would constitute a real revolution in international relations, and which would educate mankind away from its old warlike habits. The arguments against a League provided with military sanctions, which had prevailed at Paris, seemed to me only to have gained additional force with the passage of time. I felt convinced that the Dominions of the British Empire would decline to fight the wars of Central Europe in the future, and would in the last resort break away from the League rather than remain in it under such obligations. The Protocol might therefore mean a serious defection from the League, which was bound in the long run to affect the attitude even of Great Britain towards it. It was clear to me that unless the Protocol was torpedoed, it would torpedo the League, and I consider the vetoing of the Protocol after it had passed the Assembly the best service which Sir Austen Chamberlain has rendered the League, the Empire, and the world. There are no heroic short cuts to our great goal of world-peace. Mankind has to be educated into a new mentality and into a new international method, and that education is proceeding normally under the Covenant. The scrapping of the Covenant for the Protocol or anything like it would have been a real calamity.

Another serious effect of the Protocol would have been to drive the U.S.A. still farther from the League. In no conceivable way could the U.S.A. in future have taken part, directly or indirectly, in a League transformed on the Protocol basis. If the obligations of the original League were too much for the Senate to swallow, what would they have had to say of the obligations under the Protocol? How disastrous the Protocol system with its war-like commitments would have been, appears now more clearly from the declaration of the Kellogg or Paris Peace Pact, which proscribes all war as an instrument of national policy. The Peace Pact is in line with the Covenant but not with the Protocol. The Peace Pact is an advance on the Covenant, as it is intended to close up a gap which was admittedly left open in the Covenant. But if the Protocol had become the basis of our public law, the Peace Pact would not have fitted into such a system and would probably never have seen the light of day. In spite of American absence from the League, the American mind is still moving in the direction which it followed at the Peace Conference, and the importation of European ideas of military security into the

League would only have alienated America further from the League. That would have been a calamity from all conceivable points of view.

I said just now that a true and fruitful idea moves by its own momentum, and grows by opposition. The League supplies a striking illustration in support of that dictum. The United States, after having most cordially co-operated at Paris with the other Powers in working out the Covenant and in establishing the League, subsequently turned against both and declined to ratify the Covenant, for reasons of her own which it is not necessary for our purpose to discuss. Her defection was a terrible blow to the League, almost a knock-out blow, and many ardent supporters of the League were at the time seriously doubtful whether it could go on without the powerful participation of the U.S.A. Grievously crippled, the League still struggled on, made good, rendered notable service to an impoverished and distracted Europe, and gradually assisted in bringing order out of chaos. I need not recount what she did, but it was a notable record of good deeds, and its beneficent effects are being felt in all directions in the Old World. Meanwhile American abstention, which at one time had appeared to be such a grievous blow, began to assume a different aspect. America could not really wash her hands of her own work; the great ideal underlying the Covenant kept haunting her. The fair-minded and reasonable men and women of that great people felt disturbed in their conscience; they could not really be indifferent to the peace ideal;

it dominated them as it had dominated Europe. And
before long America was once more on the move,
moving forward with an immense stride on lines of
her own in support of the peace ideal. The apparent
deserter reappeared in the light of a great reinforcement at a critical moment in the struggle for world-
peace on the right lines. America is likely to become a
member of the International Court, and has initiated
a fundamental advance in the Peace Pact. What
appeared as a bad set-back in 1920 has been transformed into a resounding victory in 1928, and
America is once more in the van of the great movement towards world-peace. The League ideal has
won, and Wilson's Covenant is being completed by
the hands which tried to tear it up after the Peace.
Like the soul of John Brown, the Covenant goes
marching on, apparently benefiting as much from
defeat as from victory.

As all the members of the League, and practically
all the states outside it, have signed the Peace Pact, it
becomes part of the public law of the world. The
important question therefore arises what the effects
of the renunciation of war as an instrument of
national policy will be on the peace movement; also,
how it will affect existing international law, and
especially the law of neutrality, which was based on the
opposite concept of the legality of war. International
law since the time of Grotius has assumed that war is
a legitimate activity of states; and the law of neutrality
arose from the conception that not only was war between two or more states permissible and legitimate,

but that it was their private concern; that such a war had no interest for other parties, who consequently did not bother about its merits, and in carrying on their ordinary commerce treated both parties to it on a footing of absolute and impartial equality. On this assumption the rules of neutrality in time of war have been carefully and laboriously built up, particularly the rules relating to the capture of private property at sea, which figure under the general formula of the Freedom of the Seas. Let us endeavour for a few moments to see what the real scope of the Peace Pact is and what changes in fundamental concepts it will probably involve.

Although the Peace Pact was preceded by a lengthy international correspondence in which various Powers set forth their points of view and indicated the limits within which they were willing to renounce war, there are no reservations in the instrument itself, which in terms is an absolute acceptance of the principle of renunciation. Neither in the Pact nor in its ratification by the Powers are reservations made. Even the declaration of the United States Senate on ratification, that the Pact did not lay any legal obligations on the United States to go to the assistance of any state which might be attacked in violation of the Pact, constitutes merely a statement of fact and no reservation. So far, therefore, as the actual terms of the Pact go, it is an unconditional acceptance by practically all the states of the world of the renunciation of war as an instrument of national policy, and an unconditional undertaking to seek their rights only by peaceful means, through legal decision, arbitration, and conciliation. The Covenant left it open to a state to go to war, in case there had been no unanimous arbitral award or recommendation by the League Council in any dispute. Absence of unanimity in such a case left the position exactly as it was under the old rules of international law; either party to the dispute could legitimately resort to war; no penalty was put on it for so doing, and in case of war, the ordinary rules of neutrality applied to states who were not participants in the war. It is this opening for war which is now formally closed by the solemn and unconditional undertaking of the Peace Pact. It is, however, clear that even yet all war is not proscribed under the Pact, but only war as an instrument of national policy; in other words, private war waged by a party for its own national purposes. There remains the case of what is called public war, where a state becomes involved in war, not for its own individual ends, but for police purposes in concert with others, in pursuance of a public policy under a general instrument, such as the Covenant of the League. Thus an aggressor, who flouts a unanimous decision of the League, and goes to war, will come under the ban of the Peace Pact; other members of the League who, under the provision of Article 16 of the Covenant, subject this aggressor to an economic blockade, and in this way become involved in a war with it, will be engaged in a public war, and will not violate their undertaking under the Peace Pact. Under the Peace Pact which,

in view of its universal signature, has become the
public law of the world, there will thus in future be
two categories of war: private war, waged for individual national purposes, and public wars which are
accepted and waged as a matter of public international or police duty. Private wars are uncondi-
tionally banned and proscribed and as such can carry
no legal rights; public wars remain permissible and
legal for general police purposes and the prevention
of public violence, and carry the usual incidents of
legal warfare under the rules of international law.
Thus a state involved in a public war will lawfully
exercise as against neutrals the ordinary rights of
search and capture in accordance with international
law, while one provoking a private war will not be
entitled to these rights. The distinction between
private and public wars, which follows logically from
the provision of the Peace Pact, therefore calls for a
supplementary general convention which will clarify
the position, define private and public wars, and ex-
pressly deprive those who resort to private war of
all rights as against neutrals. By thus bringing the
sanctions of international law to bear on the position of parties resorting to private war, a very
powerful additional stimulus would be given to the
movement towards universal peace. Respectable
states are chary of going contrary to public opinion,
and they incur grave risks in so doing, as the Great
War has demonstrated. They will be far more chary
of embarking on a war which will involve their
proscription and outlawry by international law, and

their deprivation of such rights against neutrals as they have been able heretofore to exercise legally in the past. The loss of these rights would be a severe penalty and act as a deterrent in most cases against private war in future.

I would make a plea for such a convention, supplementary to the Peace Pact and carrying its general principles to their logical conclusions. The Peace Pact is only a grand beginning, and its general declarations should be followed up to their logical details. If private war is illegal, and the party resorting to it virtually a war outlaw, he must not only be deprived of all rights against neutrals, but other states should also undertake to have no dealings with him, and should not render him indirect assistance through the ordinary trade or financial channels. He should be treated as an outlaw, as a pariah among the nations; and this should be explicitly provided for. Such a convention would incidentally solve two most important problems, one affecting Anglo-American relations, the other affecting the operation of the Covenant. Let me briefly deal with these problems.

The United States has been the protagonist for neutral rights in the past, and her claim to the Freedom of the Seas remains the one great open question between the English speaking peoples, who to-day play so important a role in the affairs of the world. If this issue between them were eliminated, there is no saying how fruitful their co-operation may become in world politics, and how beneficent a part they may possibly play in the maintenance of world peace in the future. If the proscription of a war outlaw is made a reality, and if he is made to forfeit all rights of commercial intercourse while he is engaged in private war, the whole question of neutral rights is revolutionized, and the doctrine of the Freedom of the Seas ceases to be of any practical importance. If the United States had adhered to the Covenant, the doctrine would have disappeared under Article 16. I remember well President Wilson declaring at the Peace Conference that the Covenant would solve the question of the Freedom of the Seas for the future. As the United States of America did not join the League, the issue remained a live, and indeed a dangerous, one, and the time has come to eliminate it from Anglo-American relations. The Peace Pact gives the necessary opening. If the right of supply to a war outlaw is explicitly renounced, as it is implicitly renounced in the Peace Pact, the United States could no longer claim the right of a neutral to freedom of trade with such a party, and the question of Freedom of the Seas falls to the ground. The time has come to lay the ghost of this issue which has troubled the peace of the English-speaking world for more than a century. A great opening to settle it is once more given, and I hope it will not be allowed to pass without being exploited to the full.

But such a convention will have an even more important result. It will have a direct bearing on the operation of the Covenant. It will make the economic sanction under Article 16 of the Covenant a workable scheme, which it cannot be said to be at present, while the United States stands out of the League. In other words, the effect of carrying out the Peace Pact to its necessary conclusions will be the same as if the United States adhered to Article 16. For a war outlaw under the Peace Pact would in most cases be identical with an aggressor who flouted a unanimous decision of the League, and was on that account placed under the economic boycott of Article 16; and if the United States could not supply the war outlaw under the Peace Pact neither could it supply the declared aggressor under the Covenant: any peace breaker would be covered by both schemes. The carrying out of the Peace Pact to its logical conclusions would therefore mean that the economic sanction under Article 16 of the Covenant could be applied with the co-operation of the United States; and the working of the Covenant according to its original plan would at last become possible, which it has not been since the United States stood aside from the League. In a very real sense the Peace Pact thus becomes the fulfilment of the Covenant. But a supplementary convention will be necessary to remove all doubt by declaring the full and true intention of the Peace Pact. The United States need not be asked to join the League, but only to carry out in full the Peace Pact, for which it is mainly and primarily responsible. Its action will always be independent of the decisions of the League under the Covenant, but the effect will be the same, as the Covenant and the Pact will in this respect lead to the same result. The United States need not become entangled in the affairs of the League, but the operation of the Peace Pact will mean a close co-operation by the United States from its free and independent position; and for all practical purposes that will be quite enough.

One more difficulty remains. Under the Covenant and in the League there is the difficulty of determining who is an aggressor against whom the economic sanction of Article 16 should be applied. The League, in spite of much thought and trouble, has not yet found any satisfactory answer to this question. A similar difficulty will now arise under the Peace Pact. If private war breaks out, which state has resorted to it as an instrument of national policy, and should therefore incur the penalty of proscription and outlawry under the Peace Pact? It may be that in neither case is a theoretically satisfactory answer possible. But it may also prove to be unnecessary. Perhaps here, as with so many other great problems of life and action, a water-tight theory may not be arrived at. And yet a workable way may be found in practice. *Solvitur ambulando.* Let me indicate one such practical way towards world peace, which may also prove helpful in identifying and pinning down the guilty party. Under the Pacific Pact, concluded at Washington in 1921 between the Powers interested in the Pacific Ocean, it was agreed that, whenever circumstances arose which might threaten the peace, these Powers would confer with each other and concert measures for the prevention of war. The United States is a party to this Pacific Conference, and Mr. Charles E. Hughes has suggested that a similar arrangement could be applied to all situations, wherever arising, which might threaten the peace of the world. There could be no objection to the United States being party to such a General Conference system outside the League. It would include all the Powers interested in any area in which danger threatened; and in practice the Conference would in most cases prove effective in the keeping of the peace. If, in spite of all efforts, war were to break out, the question as to who is the real mischief-maker would have become clear through the work of the Conference. A Conference system similar to that under the Pacific Pact, and on more or less informal lines parallel to the League system, and including the United States and possibly Russia, may be a most useful and effective adjunct to the more elaborate peace system of the League. And the convention which I suggest for carrying out the Peace Pact might deal not only with the question of outlawry and neutrality but might also provide for such a Conference system, to which not only members of the League but also those Powers who are not League Members may adhere. In this way the unique opening given by the Peace Pact might be followed up, as it should be followed up without delay. It is America's great contribution towards world peace; it is her special approach to the greatest problem of our time and of all time, and in following it up we may therefore feel sure of her co-operation. It lays down a principle which, if sincerely carried to its logical conclusions, will take us far towards our great goal.

V

FUTURE TASKS OF THE LEAGUE

The League of Nations Union celebrated the tenth anniversary of its foundation at a peace commemoration dinner held at the Guildhall, London, on November 14. General Smuts was the chief guest, and in reply to the toast of the League of Nations spoke as follows:

V

FUTURE TASKS OF THE LEAGUE

IN the few minutes alloted to me I can only refer to a couple of points, and that in the briefest and most summary manner. But however short the time at my disposal I should not express what I feel most deeply, if I omitted to pay my small tribute to the magnificent work which the League of Nations Union has been carrying on. The educative and propaganda work of the Union has been of priceless value to the cause of peace. Its organization has been above party and cuts across all parties. It has drawn to it those men and women who really believe in world peace. To me, personally, it has been a consolation that, in the trying years behind us, South Africa could help the good cause by nominating Lord Cecil and Professor Gilbert Murray as South African representatives on the councils of the League. What these two men in particular have done for the League and this Union it would be impossible to exaggerate.

The public have helped generously with funds and must continue to help. There is to-day no better form of missionary enterprise than this service of the cause of world peace. Let us continue to make our contributions to this mission of peace and goodwill among men.

In making our money contributions to the Union we are not only helping to realize a great ideal, but we are in a very real sense paying our small insurance against the greatest danger that threatens civilization.

About the present position of the League I only wish to say this: the League has passed through many ups and downs during its first ten years. It is true that our highest hopes of ten years ago have not been realized; but neither have the dismal predictions of the critics of the League come true. On the whole it has followed a course of its own, and has quietly made good; and more recently its prospects have brightened in a very encouraging way. Germany, which was suspected and feared as a source of future danger to the League, has quite unexpectedly become an active member and a source of real strength to the League, and of support to all the good causes for which it stands. The United States, which was supposed to be indifferent, or even hostile, to the League, is going to join the World Court. The Optional Clause is at last becoming a reality, and an immense extension will thereby be given to the judicial side of the League's activities. The Peace Pact, which the United States has sponsored, has been signed, and has gone far towards closing the gap left in the Covenant. The happy conversations between the President of the United States and the British Prime Minister have given a new turn to the disarmament movement, and the forthcoming Naval Conference will open with every prospect of success. Last, not least, comes the great speech of President Hoover on Monday, November 11, which must have been read with the deepest pleasure by every supporter of the League. There was a note of

optimism in it and a ring of sincerity which are good
auguries for the future. We especially welcome the
forecast of the President that there is going to be not
merely a patch-up of the naval question on a basis of
parities and ratios, but 'a serious reduction in navies
as a relief to the economic burdens of the peoples'.
It is clear that at last business is meant with disarmament, and we look forward with the deepest interest
to the success of this policy.

In spite of all the good and hard work which has
been done, very heavy tasks confront the League. As
I understand the position to-day, there are three
great problems before the League and the whole
peace movement. The first is that of disarmament.
If a serious reduction of navies is decided upon next
January the way will be open for an attack on the more
difficult subject of military and aerial disarmament.
Of these two, aerial disarmament is the more urgent
and important, as aerial warfare constitutes by far the
more serious danger to civilization. It means ruthless
warfare not against the armed forces of the enemy but
against his civilian population, with the consequent
destruction of cities and population behind the lines.
The position with regard to air warfare is still in the
fluid, formative stage; air forces are rapidly growing
in many countries, and should therefore be dealt with
without further delay. The menace to this country
in particular from the air is more serious than any
other which it has to face. Military disarmament is
a far more thorny problem, and will probably require,
and should receive, more patient handling.

The second great problem before the League is no less important, and perhaps even more far-reaching in its bearings. It is the problem of justice. Our ideal is not merely peace, but peace with justice. There is no doubt that war has in the past sometimes served as a solvent for intolerable situations; it has sometimes destroyed the bulwarks of ancient wrong and opened the way to necessary reforms and readjustments. If war in future is to be rendered impossible, we must see to it that its function, in so far as it has been beneficent in the past, be discharged by some other means. Peace must be dynamic; it must keep the door open to reform and to freedom, and must not become an incubus on human progress. The springs of reform, of progress, and of freedom must not be frozen under a deadly peace. Peace must be the handmaiden of justice in the new world towards which mankind is marching. This position was clearly foreseen by the framers of the Covenant, and Article 19 calls for means by which obsolete or intolerable situations can be abolished. The creation of such machinery, and its careful working under proper safeguards, will be one of the greatest and most difficult tasks of the League. The time is rapidly approaching when this task will have to be faced. Otherwise all our machinery of peace, our World Court, our arbitration tribunals, and other legal agencies will merely serve to entrench the *status quo*, and render the danger of future explosions all the greater.

The third great problem before the peace movement concerns the question, what has to be done with a disturber of the peace? War may arise in future in spite of the Covenant and in spite of the Peace Pact, and, if allowed to spread, may envelop the world in flames, as we saw in the Great War. It is clear that the question of the policy to be adopted towards the aggressor, or the disturber of the peace, or the party resorting to war to further national policy, cannot be settled inside the League alone, but requires agreement between the League members and the United States. The question calls for settlement, but there is still serious disagreement as to the policy to be followed. President Hoover says that the Covenant means the application of force by other members of the League, and that the United States is confident that public opinion will suffice to check violence. But is there not a middle way open which both the League members and the United States may follow, without prejudice to their divergent viewpoints? Both have signed the Peace Pact, and are bound to see to it that this great instrument does not become a dead letter. To both, therefore, we may fairly say: Follow up the Peace Pact. Do not leave its general declaration in the air, so to say; but carry it to its reasonable conclusion. If that is done, it may be found, as I pointed out at Oxford last Saturday,[1] that important changes in international law will become necessary, which will render the position of the violator of the Peace Pact untenable, if not impossible. There will be no question of the application of force, but there

---

[1] Pp. 130–7.

will be consequential changes of the laws of neutrality which will have the most far-reaching results, both for future peace and for the settlement of current controversies. The Peace Pact with its far-reaching implications not only affords an unrivalled opportunity for the strengthening of the peace position; it also offers a bridge between the divergent views on peace methods held on both sides of the Atlantic. This unique opportunity should therefore be exploited to the full.

I confess that I am doubtful about the suggestion of the President in reference to the immunity of food ships. I doubt whether methods of humanizing private war will ever really serve a useful purpose. That was the road followed in the era preceding the Great War. As soon, however, as the first shot was fired these humanizing expedients went by the board. It will always be so. War cannot be effectively humanized; its utter inhumanity and inexpressible barbarity will be its undoing and will work the cure, and not attempts at rendering it more humane to the innocent. The axe has been laid to the root of the tree; let us keep hewing there. Under the Peace Pact mankind has definitely and unanimously declared war against war. Let us not in any way weaken or recede from that position.

Let us develop the conference system, both for members and non-members of the League. The spirit of conference is the very soul of the peace movement. Such conferences will in most cases prove effective in keeping the peace, and if war should break out they will disclose the mischief-maker. Such conferences may also lead to concerted action in regard to any special immunities for food ships and the like, under very exceptional circumstances which may arise. But no general rules should be laid down in advance, which will make the way of the transgressor easier for the future.

VI
DEMOCRACY

VI

DEMOCRACY [1]

THIS visit to Cambridge is a great occasion for me, and I look upon it as an honour and a privilege. I could not have come to lecture before the sister university without also paying a visit to my Alma Mater; natural piety and the great memories of the past alone would have prevented that. I was therefore grateful for the invitation of the Principal of Newnham College to come and deliver the Sidgwick Memorial lecture this term, as it gave me the welcome opportunity for this visit and of addressing my friends in my old university.

My memory goes back to the Cambridge of a generation ago, in which Henry Sidgwick was one of the foremost figures. I had not the advantage of attending his courses on philosophy, and have regretted this ever since, in proportion as my own interest in philosophical subjects has deepened. But I followed his course on politics, and this must be my excuse for taking a political theme for my lecture to-day. Sidgwick had not only a singularly acute mind, but very wide intellectual and social sympathies, which dominated his outlook on life, and made his philosophy in a large measure subservient to social service in the widest sense. Hence his unremitting efforts for University reform; hence his

[1] Sidgwick Memorial Lecture, delivered at Newnham College, Cambridge, on 30 November 1929.

continuous efforts on behalf of women's education, and his great work in connexion with the foundation and progress of this College. Hence also his interest in politics, both in its theoretical and practical aspects. Although his highly critical mind made him averse to all catchwords and popular phrases, he was a convinced believer in political liberty, and in the institutions to which it has given birth in the modern world. A brief discussion of the present position of Democracy would therefore not be out of place in a memorial lecture, and it might serve a useful purpose in drawing attention to one or two of the changes in political institutions, to which the present tendencies seem to point. Democracy is no longer accepted at its face value, and its institutions are being more and more subjected to hostile, and even destructive, criticism. A summary review of a few of its main features in the brief time at my disposal may therefore not be inappropriate or devoid of value.

In one of his most famous and resounding phrases, Woodrow Wilson declared that the Great War was being fought to make the world safe for democracy. Events since the Great War have raised the question, however, in many quarters whether democracy is safe for the world. There has been a widespread disillusion over democracy; over half of Europe it has ceased to function as the mainspring of political institutions, and its place has been taken by forms of dictatorship, either of the one or the minority, which are a negation of the essence of democracy. Nor can it be said that these substitutes for democracy promise to be a real improvement on it. Bolshevism in Russia, whatever its future may be, has proved to be one of the most destructive experiments in history, and has led to more human misery and to greater economic and industrial decay than would have been thought possible in a great European community. Fascism in Italy, again, in spite of its temporary success, resembles nothing so much as Vesuvius in one of its periods of quiescence; anxiety over what will happen next spoils the doubtful satisfaction over the present. The fact is that, while there is great and widespread dissatisfaction with present political democracy, no better alternative as a basis of government has yet presented itself, and the politically more advanced democracies of the world continue to move on the old lines, more from a sense of convenience, however, than from conviction. The active co-operation of the governed in their government still holds the field as the first axiom of political philosophy. But a subtle change is coming over the scene. With all the far-reaching changes taking place in all departments of life and thought, political institutions are in a sense also in the melting-pot. Human government seems to be outgrowing its political clothes; social and political needs are changing, political fashions are changing, and there is a growing spirit of unrest in the air, and a growing readiness to make political experiments. There is no doubt that mankind—at least politically-conscious mankind—is switching over, in some countries violently, and in others more quietly and constitutionally, from the old to new lines in political government, and a great deal of fundamental thinking will be required to make the change over as frictionless as possible.

The most far-reaching change which is taking place to-day in human affairs is in the sphere of international relations; but it will not remain confined to those relations. The international is taking its place alongside of the national in the affairs of mankind. Hitherto human government has been moving on national lines, and international relations have been subsidiary, a sort of by-product of the national situation. But a change is coming in this subordinate status of the international. The League of Nations is the great new fact, and its ideal of the abolition of war as an instrument of national policy, which is now taking firm shape, is going to transform the national situation, and in the end to remould the forms as well as the spirit of national government. This is perhaps not yet realized, except very vaguely, and it may be useful to consider more closely the essential difference between the existing national and the growing international system.

The difference is not between state and super-state, as it is sometimes put. The League of Nations is not the beginnings of a superstate which is destined to swallow the present national states, and in that way to abolish nationalism. That has not been the conception of its founders, and if any such development is ever to take place in future, the present basis of the League will have to be radically recast. The

League was not conceived or founded to function as a superstate. For that, its constitution would have to be quite different. It presupposes the national states and their continued existence. It is at present no more than an honest broker between states; a liaison of a new, regular, authoritative character. It does not displace states, but puts itself in the gap between them. It becomes the buffer which receives the shocks and absorbs the differences. At present it is only the wise broad-minded circumspect counsellor of kings. If in the end it becomes more, if in time the wise counsellor becomes the Prime Minister, whose advice is bound to be followed, that will be an unforeseen and unprovided-for development, and in any case it is so remote a contingency that we need not trouble about it to-day. The great change for the future will not be due to the status or the structure of the League as a superstate, which it is not, but to its functions as the pacificator, preventing wars and removing causes of differences between states.

Let us consider for a moment what that means. War is, or at least has been, the chief instrument of national policy. The state has been defined as the worship of power. The greatness and power of the state is the pride and the ideal of its citizens, for which they are prepared to sacrifice their property and, in the last resort, their lives. The state incarnates the passion of nationalism which has been the most powerful factor in modern history; and the last and chief weapon of the national state is war. In the competition for aggrandizement and power between states, there is in the last resort no other arbiter but war. War as an instrument of national policy becomes all-important to the state; the glory of the state means the glorification of war. Owing to the absence in modern times of all other machinery to mediate between states, the role of war has become dominant, and war has in a large measure written the history of the world. The ridicule poured on text-books of history because of the emphasis they lay on wars has not been really justified. The importance of war has not been exaggerated; the text-books have only gone astray in neglecting other important factors. War was the greatest act of state of the nations; and it was war that made peace between them. We have seen a most illuminating illustration of that in our own time. The Versailles Peace was the latest, let us pray that it will remain the last, chief political act of the old order—in fact the final act of the old war system, which has prevailed throughout history. Those who looked upon the Peace of 1919 as the new beginning, the foundation of the new world, expected too much. It was only by a miracle that the Peace Treaty contained the seeds of the new order which was to arise in the world. The first chapter of the Peace Treaty, containing the Covenant of the League, was an anachronism from the point of view of the whole instrument. At that one point, and there only, the new spirit burst through the old shell. Everywhere else we had a peace which was the consummation of the war. In that last supreme effort of the national system, with governments and leaders such as the war had thrown up, only a War peace could be expected, and that we got at Versailles. It was the last and ripest fruit of the old system. Settlement by war, war as the instrument of national policy; and a peace which reflected the mentality in which the war had been fought and which garnered its fruits: such was the old system, as it existed in 1919 and as it had existed from the beginning. The important point is that war was the very essence of the old system. In the great clashes of national ambitions, inflamed and rendered implacable by national passions and sufferings and injustices, there was really nothing else to decide under the old system but power—the power of the sword.

From this it follows that, if war as an instrument of national policy is to disappear, the influence of national passions in international affairs will have to be seriously moderated and as far as possible eliminated. War is the child of national passions, of an inflamed unwholesome mentality, springing from groundless or exaggerated fears or ambitions, usually from both combined. The most effective means of preventing war would be the cure of this national soul-sickness; or if it could not be cured outright, it could at least be moderated, and its baneful influence on international relations rendered less effective. Of course, the sense of security against war would be the best antidote to this disease. If the conviction becomes general that the League, and the influences behind it, can be relied on to keep the peace, both the fear of aggression and the ambition for aggrandizement would abate of themselves, and the inflammation which causes war would naturally subside. Our best efforts should therefore be directed towards making the League a reality, towards increasing its authority and prestige, and thus towards strengthening the atmosphere of security, in which the danger of war would of itself diminish and eventually disappear. The peaceful mentality could best be created by increasing the popular faith in the League, the general conviction that it is not a make-believe but a growing reality in the life of the world. The continual decrying of the League in certain quarters, the occasional failure of the League to rise to the occasion, the continued maintenance of bloated armaments even by those who profess to believe in the League, all combine to shake public confidence in it, to injure its credit and prestige, and to keep alive that atmosphere of uncertainty and fear which breeds the pest of war. While everything should be done by the Powers to support the League in its difficult task and to bring success to its endeavours, the organs of public opinion, the press and parliament and pulpit, should give it their warm support. Most important of all, an atmosphere favourable to the League and a peaceful co-operative international order should be fostered among the young, and especially through the school curriculum.

During the ten years of its existence the League has made great progress, and its prestige is to-day happily very different from what it was in its first

years. This progress should be maintained at all
costs for the future. But although improvement and
progress are possible along these lines, it would not
be wise to rely on this possibility alone. It will take
a long time for the fires that smoulder in the Old
World to die down; and these fires are still continually being fanned by an irresponsible press and
powerful interests. It is still so easy to mislead and
delude the public by playing on their national
passions that it will not be safe to rely on the growth
of a favourable mentality alone for the maintenance
of world-peace. We should look also to other means
of diminishing the pressure which unwholesome
national sentiment may exert on affairs. National
sentiment in international relations should no longer
play such an overwhelming part, and means should
be found through new institutions to moderate its
excessive influence. I am going to suggest such an
institution or new organ of government. And in my
opinion it is all the more urgently called for, because
something is wanted to counteract new disturbing
influences which are appearing in the state to-day.
For while the peace movement of our day calls
for a real advance in public opinion, other contem-
porary movements appear to be in an opposite
direction. The wise guidance of public opinion
becomes ever more difficult and uncertain.

Owing to the spread of education and the reading
habit, the pervasive influence of the press and the
kinema, and numerous other forms of public and
private propaganda, the massed force of public

opinion is every day becoming greater and more incalculable, and to politicians more terrifying. It is no longer the elected representatives of the people who mainly guide and interpret the popular mind in matters political. The politician to-day often plays a quite minor role in the formation and guidance of public opinion. He is often more a puppet than a guide in public affairs. Compared to the other younger more virile organs of public opinion, parliament itself is becoming of less and less importance. This is notoriously the case even in constitutionally governed countries, while in others parliament, except as a form, has disappeared. Universal suffrage has not improved our type of legislator. While the growing intricacy of public questions makes politics an all-time job calling for great knowledge and devotion, the electorate not uncommonly chooses the more shallow and showy type of amateur who can be most profuse in promises. This has affected the position and character of parliament. From an attitude of respect to parliament, the public have passed to one of indifference and boredom. Political meetings also have altered their character, and are often attended more for the by-play and the fun than for serious discussion or political enlightenment; and this change is reflected in the scrappy press reports of such meetings. With this change in public opinion has gone a change in the status of public men of which they are only too conscious themselves. They are aware that they do not count any more in the old way, that their prestige has suffered and their influence on affairs has declined. In spite of the continuance of the old parliamentary forms, their authority is no longer what it was. As a consequence their old sense of confidence and responsibility has also declined. There is thus a subtle change of values which is acting like a solvent on the old democratic ideas. It is not so much criticism or attack of representative institutions which has done the damage; there has been an impalpable change in the public mind, and the organs and institutions and personnel of human government have insensibly depreciated in popular values. In this loss of authority they suffer with most of the other institutions of our civilization. Authority is no longer accepted as an unquestioned fact and at its face value; it is asked for its credentials or, what is worse, it is simply passed by silently and ignored. It is true that government has suffered less in prestige than parliament, and the decline of parliament has even tended to concentrate more responsibility and power in the hands of government. But even so, statesmen do not feel on as firm ground as formerly; they have lost the old sense of security before the new incalculable forces and movements of public opinion. In this uncertainty and bewilderment they are often less inclined to stand up to the vagaries of public opinion; their self-confidence has been undermined, and the tendency to move with the tide of opinion is more pronounced than before. While the situation calls for supermen, the uncertainties and vacillations of public opinion seem in fact to have a paralysing effect, and to lead to more opportunism and drifting. This is the case not only in domestic affairs, but also in the domain of international affairs. In this arena, which has always been dominated by the national passions—the fears, suspicions, and ambitions of the nations—the position has become more difficult than ever, owing to the vastly increased force and volume of public opinion. And leadership to meet this situation has on the whole weakened; statesmen, even the most powerful and influential, show less inclination to stand up to the passions of their peoples than before. There was for instance more courage shown at the Congress of Vienna after the Napoleonic War than at Versailles after the Great War. The press was less vocal and public opinion was less inflamed and violent. Politicians to-day are often baffled and almost paralysed by the incalculable forces of public opinion that surround them. The position therefore often arises that in very difficult situations the politicians as the representatives of public opinion have to be cut out, and the handling of the problems entrusted to impartial experts who are not dependent on public opinion.

As an instance, I may mention the Reparation question, which has had to be removed from the venue of politics, has had to be taken away from the diplomats and the statesmen, and entrusted to a committee of financial and economic experts. Experts are not dominated by and dependent on public opinion in the same way as the statesmen. They are of course fully aware of the state of feeling among their peoples, they may even share that feeling to a large extent. But they are not dependent on that feeling, and they are first and foremost dominated by a sense of the facts, by a profound knowledge of what is financially possible, and by scientific principles which transcend the desires of men. And in dealing with a situation, which is not merely surrounded by intense popular feelings and illusions, but which above all calls for knowledge of fixed principles and for expert skill, they have successfully pointed out the way which the statesmen have had largely to follow. The Dawes and Young Commissions were not only valuable because of the great work they did, but even more so because they are typical of a new method of dealing with such questions. In the storm and stress of our time, a new mechanism is thus being evolved and put into the vast growing machine of human government. Of course there is nothing new in commissions; it is an old dodge of governments to meet awkward or complicated situations with a Royal Commission. But the Dawes and Young Commissions differ from such bodies in many important respects. They actually tackled a problem which had repeatedly been before governments and had been found to be insoluble by them. They applied the forces of science and expert skill and wisdom to a problem which had been hopelessly vitiated by human prejudice. And they succeeded in finding a solution, however temporary in character it may prove to be. These Commissions marshalled the new forces of science against the forces of popular sentiment; the battle took place, not in the calm regions of science but in the storm area of politics where passion had usually been victorious. And in that battle science won a victory, not only notable in itself, but far-reaching as a pointer on the future road of human government. Democracy is not enough. The fierce and implacable spirit of nationalism, of national egoism, which democracy incidentally represents, is not enough. National egoism and war are twin sister and brother. If war is to go, the other must go too, or at least its malign influence in the affairs of the world must be abated or neutralized. To make the new peace order function successfully, it is necessary to provide for new machinery which will be less directly under the pressure of public opinion than the politicians are, and needs must be, in a democratic state.

The position here is entirely paralleled by the development historically of peace and good order within the state or the nation. To suppress private feuds and vendettas or factional disturbances within the nation a system of resort to judicial experts was evolved. The decision of the quarrel was entrusted to men of recognized ability and impartiality, wise men skilled in the law and clothed by public opinion with the necessary authority. Private peace is based on the finding of the judicial expert, who does not enforce his own judgement; he leaves it to the government or executive power to carry it out; but its execution by the government becomes in course of time the accepted routine. In the same way the

new peace system of the nations necessitates a resort
to the impartial judicial or scientific expert. Highly
trained experts, with wide experience of affairs, and
standing aloof from the political game, are called in
to declare the principles of settlement, leaving it to
the national governments, separately or in conference,
to carry them out. In the new order of things this has
become necessary machinery, just as necessary probably as are the law courts in a state, if justice and
fairplay are to prevail between nations, and the undue
influence of national passions is to be eliminated from
the settlement of international differences. It is only
the novelty of the matter which makes us fail to
appreciate its far-reaching importance for the future,
and its necessity for the normal functioning of the
new peace system. But the beginning has been made,
fitfully and sporadically it is true; but in course of
time the precedent of to-day will become the basis of
the regular routine and the normal procedure of the
nations in their common affairs. Just as kings and
statesmen were not enough for the affairs of the
nation, and judges became necessary to declare and
apply the law, so statesmen are not enough to solve
the problems which arise in international affairs.
The national passions on which they are dependent
for power, and the mass complexes often dominating
and blinding the popular mind, leave them no real
chance and make wise action most difficult. The one
statesman at the Peace Conference who took his
courage in both hands and saw his great ideal
through, was immediately afterwards broken on the

wheel by the greatest democracy of the world. It is
not fair to expect the impossible from men who
represent, first and foremost, not abstract ideals, but
their own peoples with their national view-points and
prejudices. The nations must become accustomed to
look to the organized system of the expert report
which gives a just and impartial lead to governments
and public opinion, and which should be regularly
accepted just as judicial decisions are accepted as a
matter of course. The Permanent Court of International Justice, acting within the purely legal
domain, should be paralleled by a system of expert
international advisers, who will have no executive
power, but whose authority in the domain of applied
science, finance, and all the vastly intricate problems
which confront the modern world, will be as readily
accepted and will be as unquestioned as that of the
International Court itself.

The matter may be put in an even wider historic
and scientific setting. Judicial institutions arose in
human society because law was the only science in
which expertness was recognized at that early date.
Religion was left to the priestly order, who in the still
undifferentiated domain of theology, magic, and medicine had unquestioned authority. From this theo-
cratic complex, law was early segregated as the first
science standing by itself and demanding an institution of its own. This segregation was of course
entirely due to the lawlessness and feuds existing
within the community, and the necessity to compose
them. Wise men, skilled in the customs of the tribe

and in its ancient lore, came to be recognized as authorities, and were called in to handle the quarrels of the families and the groups. And in time these skilled exponents of the law of the tribe became the judges and the tribunals to decide disputes and settle differences within the tribe, and later within the nation or state. Thus law arose as the first science and was recognized by the state in an authoritative way. Law is the oldest but no longer the only science. The rise of the sciences, of Science, is the most out-standing fact of the modern world, and has led to the most far-reaching changes in human view-points, in human betterment, in individual and national power. Eventually it will lead to the greatest changes in human government. The rise has been so sudden that our political institutions have not yet had time even to begin adjusting themselves to the new situation. But science is necessary to the modern state and should have its functional relation to the state. Not only the discoveries of science, but the mature, sober, impartial spirit of science is what is above all else necessary for the functioning of the modern state, and of the new international system. Science is first and foremost an attitude, an outlook, a method of acquir-ing knowledge, and in the second place it is a body of results and truths. In both respects science is essential to the working of the state. The discoveries and teachings of science are the most powerful weapons with which man is fighting to-day the battle of life, and overcoming the evils and the drawbacks that beset our human lot, and this all-important fact should be reflected in our system of government. In view of all this it is a curious fact that science is not yet an organized government service anywhere in the world. I have, however, no doubt that the rapidly growing influence of science in all departments of human activity and of government will yet lead to a far more important place for science in the organization of the state in future. It may yet become the governing factor in our human organization, whether that organization will take the form of government or something better than government which may evolve in course of time. But apart from the power and results of science, we want to-day the scientific spirit in human affairs. Its method is that of complete impartiality and absolute respect for fact and for truth. Human desires do not enter into the purview of the scientist in trying to solve a natural problem. Philosophers have attributed a moral indifference to nature: I think wrongly. But there is an emotional indifference of science, which is its very essence and ideal. Emotions, desires, passions carry no weight in the balance of science. Illusions do not count with science. Science is cured of the childish belief that what is desired must be true or must exist; hence I have spoken of the maturity of the scientific spirit. It is this spirit which above all is to-day called for in the administration of human affairs. As justice is said to be blind, so science is deaf and blind to illusion and passion; it deals with facts on their merits. And as applied to human affairs it means the sober pursuit of the truth, the single desire to know things as they are, and to assign values according to the facts; to find solutions which will be in accord with nature's laws, and not the dictates of human self-interest. To me there is something divine in this lofty ideal which is the very essence of science. The application of the true scientific spirit to human affairs, if it were humanly possible, would mean such a reign of justice and fair play on earth as only poets have dreamt of. The cool, serious, gentle spirit of science is, above all, wanted in the storm-tossed domain of international affairs. And the scientific expert, for whom I am pleading as a regular institution in public affairs, may prove a most valuable link in the international organization of the future. He will function normally and dispassionately, whatever international storm may rage outside; and his findings will be quietly accepted in the end, as the higher wisdom and the better way.

But it is not only in international affairs that this new link of the scientific expert is called for. If Democracy is to last it will have to be introduced also into our system of national government. As I have already explained, the power of the Press and of other forms of publicity is leading to such an inflation of public opinion and popular and party passions, that statesmen have comparatively little scope nowadays, and find it more and more difficult to impose their wills. As a result we have governmental drift, stagnation, and impotence. By a direct road we march to Fascism and the like. Men will not sit down under intolerable evils simply because their government is supine. These dubious expedients are resorted to when government does not function normally and wholesomely; and the impotence of the government is often due, not so much to the people, as to a serious defect in the machinery of government. A moderator or regulator ought to be introduced which will tone down democratic excesses in a way which the political government is not capable of. It ought to become recognized that the scientific political expert is a necessary institution in national government. Great party disputes, which threaten the tranquillity or the progress of the state, should be remitted to a body of experts, whose personal characters and reputations confer exceptional authority on them, and whose recommendations should be available as a guide for public opinion and the government. Between the public, played upon and worked up by a storm of public opinion on the one hand, and the popular leaders on the other, should be interpolated this new institution of expert scientific advisers, who will moderate the public excitement, and bring the question in issue down to the bed-rock of fact. Where the government has to fight the fires of public opinion single-handed, and heroically does its duty, it usually gets burnt in the end, and punished by the loss of public favour. It gets punished, not for its sins but for its virtues, and its enemies rule in its place. The inevitable effect must be a weakening of the sense of responsibility in public men, an inclination cynically to move with the tide, to 'dish' one's opponents and remain in office a little longer. Hence weakness, vacillation, opportunism take the place of real courageous statesmanship, and all good causes suffer because of the defects of the democratic system.

To students of politics it must be evident that there is already a strong tendency in the direction I am advocating. Knotty industrial questions with a strong political taint are tending more and more to be remitted to expert inquiry. But it is necessary for the adoption of the new system that these inquiries should become more systematic and regularized, and that commissions of inquiry should be most carefully and impartially chosen, and their recommendations carried out, unless there is the strongest case to the contrary. The failure for reasons of party policy to carry out such recommendations makes the new system impossible, and often leads to disastrous consequences, as you will know from many recent instances which I need not mention.

Apart from the factors already noticed, the work of government is rendered more difficult to-day by the unprecedented concentration of tasks with which it is confronted. The task of administration is very different from what it was even a generation ago. The sphere of government activities has extended enormously, its duties have multiplied in all directions, and the new work is largely of an intricate and complex character. The burden is continually growing owing to demands for new services, and it is overtaxing the capacity of the old machine. The machine becomes heavy and cumbrous, the wheels become clogged and cease to go round with normal smoothness. The whole system of government tends to become top-heavy and to get out of gear. The machine has to be continually overhauled and brought up to date. We often blame the personnel when we should rather blame the out-of-date machine which they are called upon to work. In political policy, too, it is sometimes less the spirit of the people than faulty methods that makes for failure. I am optimist enough to believe that there is on the whole and in the long run sufficient good sense and practical wisdom in the people to make for good government and sound policy. There are of course moments of aberration, occasions when one or other section of the people seems to lose their heads, and things are done for which it, as well as the nation, pays dearly. But these are the exceptional lapses from habitual good sense. On the whole a well-trained European community can be safely trusted to do the best for itself under normal circumstances. If things go wrong, it is often the wrong political method that has been pursued, or a faulty institution that has functioned. Political institutions often make all the difference between good and bad government. A people may have the sense of what is right, and desire to follow it, and yet inadequate institutions may stultify that desire. The rules of procedure and debate in a legislature, for instance, may reduce it to impotence. Society is in its essence dynamic and organic, and our political institutions require continual reshaping if we wish to get good results out of them. The fundamental principles of government, the ground-plan of the democratic system, may be quite sound, but the detailed organization may become out of date. In that way the breakdown comes about. The city-state of antiquity, with the direct participation of all citizens in the assembly, succeeded for a time in producing the most wonderful results. But the time came when, with the extension of state activities beyond the bounds of the city, the multitude of counsellors only produced embarrassment, indecision, and inefficiency, and finally led to a complete breakdown, and a reversion to the old tyrannies.

The nation-state of the modern world, again, with its indirect representation and parliamentary system, has functioned very well up to recent years, but is now becoming a much more difficult machine to work, owing to universal suffrage, the mass movements of public opinion, the multiplication of governmental activities, and the immense complication of modern industrial and other conditions. The men to direct and work so great a machine are not easy to find, and yet the people are supposed to find them with the crudest means of popular choice. The wrong men are often selected; and even if the right men rise to the top, they are often inexperienced, and are not there long enough to learn to run their complicated job properly. Hence the risk of inertia and drift, perhaps one of the greatest dangers before the government of to-day. Urgent problems clamour in all directions, but the good man is absent or delays; and the job is in consequence entrusted to the blundering improvisor and the 'chancer', whose methods of hustle and noise appeal to the people, and especially to the sensational press.

It is evident that under such conditions very great power becomes concentrated in the hands of the civil service. This power behind the throne has been steadily growing in influence with the rise of the modern state and the growing complication of the functions of government. Beneficent if kept under proper control, it becomes an unmitigated bureaucracy if it assumes control itself, as it tends to do under weak and rapidly changing governments. In some European countries, and notably in Russia, the bureaucracy has been the real cause of revolution. The uncontrolled service ceases to be the loyal servant, and becomes parasitical on the country; even governments become its puppets, and in the end it comes to exercise authority for its own ends, and not for the public good. An ideal public service would go far to supply the deficiencies of democratic government, with its vacillation and inexpertness. But in the complicated organism of the state, any organ which becomes independent of the rest becomes a danger, and nothing is so dangerous to the state as a public service which does not march with the people, and becomes a drag on well-ordered progress; it may even have to be dynamited out of its fixed position. Against the growing tendency towards bureaucracy in the public service, only strong governments can protect the people, and democracy does not, under present conditions, tend to produce strong governments. And so the vicious circle continues. Human

government can be no better in the end than human
nature, and popular self-government will continue to
be a difficult machine to work in practice, until the
political education of the people has reached a very
much higher level.

The end of government is not merely good government, but the education of the people in good government, its self-education in running its own affairs.
Even at the price of less efficient government let the
people by all means gain its own experience and
develop its own capacity for self-government. The
short cuts do not really bring us much farther, except
to the next turn of the wheel of revolution. Liberty
as a form of political government is a difficult experiment, and it is not without its dangers, as I have
pointed out. But it is at any rate less dangerous than
its alternatives, and under modern conditions it is
probably the only political system that promises to
endure. The consent of the governed is the only
secure and lasting basis of government, and liberty is
the condition of consent. Only free men can consent
to their form of government. Where there is no freedom and no consent, there must be a basis of force;
the one or the minority in control can keep the
majority in check only by means of force or domination, which is utterly repugnant to the new tendencies
which are shaping political developments to-day.
Bolshevism and Fascism, which are the current alternatives to democratic liberty, may be defended as a
way out of intolerable situations, but they are temporary expedients, often tried and discarded before,

and they will be discarded again after the present trials. The only political philosophy which holds the field is that which recognizes the fundamental ideals of human life in human government, and of these the greatest is liberty. No enduring system can be established on the negation of liberty, even if it comes with the temporary gift of good government. This elementary fact needs no labouring with an English audience.

To sum up therefore. Political democracy, as a principle of human government, is in essence unassailable, and will continue to be the fundamental political faith of all advanced peoples. But the time-honoured institutions of democracy stand on a less secure footing. Various important factors are making for a change in the old organization. There is in the first place the growing complication in the character and functions of the modern state, which calls for a far greater element of scientific expertness in its personnel. There is in the second place a far greater mobilization of public opinion through the Press, the kinema, and the thousand and one other forms of publicity which to-day make the work of the statesman much more difficult than before. Publicity is becoming an almost greater evil than secret diplomacy was formerly. It gives a power to the Press and to all forms of scaremongering which rivals that of governments and becomes a grave menace to government. Those who are in temporary command of public opinion wield a power and an influence, both in national and international affairs, which may seriously interfere with the efficiency of government and the promotion of international goodwill. Against this new invasion the old forms of democratic government require reinforcement from the reasonable and educated sections of the community. Universal suffrage has to be tempered with universal science. The forces of science have to be mobilized against the mob forces of publicity. This could best be done by following up the precedent, already repeatedly tried with success in recent years, of expert scientific commissions to deal with complicated national and international issues, which have to be removed from the party or partisan arena. The scientific economic expert should come to play in the modern state, and in international relations, a part somewhat analogous to that of the legal expert and the law court, and thus ease the responsibility of government in matters with which it is less fitted to deal. Already there is a strong tendency among big industrial and economic interests to cut out the government, and to seek the solution of their troubles away from the political interference of the government. The meaning of it all is that both the organization and the functioning of the state should become more scientific, impartial, businesslike, and less purely political in the old sense. The scientific expert should come in as a new additional organ of the modern democratic state.

Finally, the ideal of the abolition of war as an instrument of national policy deprives national governments of what has been their last refuge in the past; they can no longer appeal to this great weapon of

A a

kings, and must in future organize their resources on a peace footing, and submit their quarrels to the tribunal of the nations. The favourite old dodge of avoiding internal trouble by embarking on foreign adventure can no longer be resorted to. Deprived of all means of external aggrandizement, the state becomes an organization for the peaceful self-development and perfection of citizenship on a basis which will more and more tend to be universal, and not merely national. Its character will thus be profoundly transformed, but the universal human ideals, which have in the past suffered in the clash of national egoisms and of war, will have freer scope and fuller realization than before. The democratic ideal fits in with the peaceful international régime of the future and is in no real danger from it.

I have occupied your time largely with a discussion of the changing institutions of democracy. But I wish in conclusion to point out that democracy in the last resort depends, not so much on machinery of government, as on the spirit of a people, on its unexhausted and growing fund of goodwill and understanding, on its capacity for social magnanimity and unselfish service. In proportion as this spiritual and scientific humanism becomes diffused throughout all classes of the nation, only in that proportion will the right atmosphere for democracy exist. It will be largely the function of the universities to foster this culture and promote this high spirit of social service and understanding. It will be pre-eminently the task of the universities to train the future leaders of democracy.

Through humanism, through science, by the culture
of the spirit and the ideals of the higher life, the
universities will equip the coming generations for
their duties of leadership. The universities will thus
come to play an ever more important role in the life
of the nation, and will become the real spiritual home
of its leaders. The young men and women coming
from it will carry into national life and government
that indefinable something which is more precious
than all the organs and institutions of society. And
only in proportion as they do this will human self-
government come into its own.

INDEX

Abyssinia, 14, 24, 27, 44.
Act of Union, 97.
Africa: 'Africa for the Africans', 45, 49; 'Africa will still remain Africa', 33–4; agriculture, 43, 81–3, 90; Africa and the Great War, 24–6; Annual Conference on African Problems, 68; anthropology in Africa, 86; camel transport, 28; Christianity, 52–4, 86; civil servants, 54–5; communication and transport, 27–8; education, 90; equal political rights, 94–8; exploration, 4 sqq.; political aspects of exploration, 22–3; industrial development, 24; industrial segregation impracticable, 93–4; international congresses, 22, 23; intoxicating liquors, 90; labour, compulsory or indentured, 45, 46; land settlement, 67; land tenure and cultivation, 80–3, 90; mandates, 88–9; missionary work, 32–3, 52–4, 85; medical missions, 53; mines, 40–2; motor transport, 27–8; native administration, 90, 102; Native Affairs Commission, 85; native migration, 65, 90, 99, 100; native policy, 73–103; native political rights, 94–8; native population, 59; native self-government, 84, 90–1; native tribal authority, 86–90; natives, characteristics of, 47, 75–6; partition of Africa, 23–5; racial problems, 30–1; railway communication, 27; segregation, 92–4, 98–103; settlement, 37–69; slavery, 5, 12, 13, 16, 23, 45, 46, 77; taxation, 46, 80, 81, 82, 84, 89; water pollution, 90; white settlement and employment, 45–55, 63–9, 80–1, 99–101; and native land rights, 55–60; *see also* Livingstone, David.
British Africa, external trade, 31–2.

Central Africa, agricultural advances in, 31.
East Africa, 29, 55–8, 62, 66, 67; British policy in, 49; external trade, 31–2; settlement of, 43–4; white settlement, 50; German East African campaign, 25; Governors of East African Territories on European settlement, 57–8.
North-West Africa, 27.
South Africa, 4 sqq., 60, 82–5, 88, 92, 94, 97, 98, 101, 141; mining, 28–31; Scots in South Africa, 3, 4, 7; white population, 41; Union of, 27, 39, 68.
South-West Africa, 27, 61.
West Africa, 54–8; external trade of British West Africa, 31–2.
Albert Edward, Lake, 21.
Albert Nyanza, Lake, 21, 27.
Andersson, 7.
Angola, 10, 12, 27, 29, 59.
Aruwimi, River, 21.
Aryans, 30.
Asia and Europe, 73–4.
Australian Institute of Tropical Medicine, 61.

Bagirmi, 20.
Bahr el Ghazal, 20.
Baker, Sir Samuel, 14.
Bangweolo, Lake, 7, 17, 19, 22.
Bantu, the, 74, 75.
Barth, Henry, 7.
Bechuana, Livingstone's mission at, 7.
Bechuanaland, 9.
Belgium, 24, 25.
Benguella, 19.
Berlin African Conference (1885), 23.
Bolshevism, 153, 175.
Borden, Sir Robert, 37.
Bruce, James, 7.
Brussels International African Conference, 22.

PRINTED IN GREAT BRITAIN AT THE UNIVERSITY PRESS, OXFORD
BY JOHN JOHNSON, PRINTER TO THE UNIVERSITY

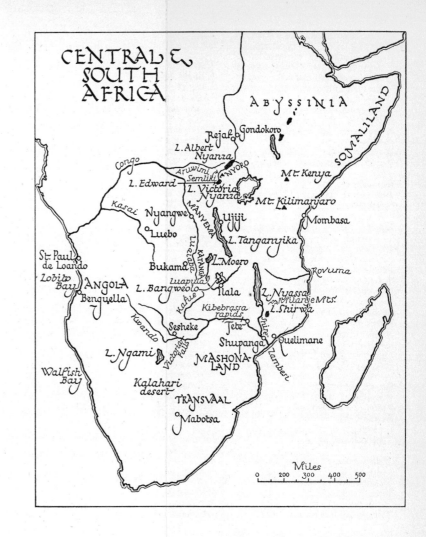

CENTRAL &
SOUTH
AFRICA

ABYSSINIA

SOMALILAND

Rejaf Gondokoro
L. Albert
Nyanza
UNYORO

Congo
Aruwimi
Semliki
L. Edward
L. Victoria
Nyanza

Mt. Kenya

Mt. Kilimanjaro

Kasai
Nyangwe
Luebo
Ujiji
Mombasa

St. Paul
de Loando
Lobito
Bay
ANGOLA
Benguella

Bukama
L. Moero

L. Tanganyika

Rovuma

Luapula
L. Bangweolo
Kafue
Ilala

L. Nyassa
Milanje Mts.
L. Shirwa

Kibebrassa
rapids

Kwando
Sesheke
Tete
Shupanga
Quelimane

Zambesi

L. Ngami
Victoria
Falls
MASHONA-
LAND

Walfish
Bay

Kalahari
desert
TRANSVAAL

Mabotsa

Miles
0   200   300   400   500